The Atlanta Campaign

The Atlanta Campaign

May - November, 1864

John Cannan

COMBINED BOOKS

To Mom and Pop

Copyright © 1991 by John Cannan

All rights reserved. No part of this publication may be reproduced, stored in a retrieval system or transmitted in any form or by any means, electrical, mechanical or otherwise without first seeking the written permission of the Publisher.

First published in the United States of America in 1991 by Combined Books, Inc.

For information, address:
Combined Books, Inc.
151 East 10th Avenue
Conshohocken, PA 19428

Library of Congress Cataloging-in-Publication Data available

ISBN 0-938289-05-5

Printed in Hong Kong.

Acknowledgements

Many thanks to Art Yao, Tanjam Narasimhan, Carol Breedlove, Teresa Cannan and Francesca Cannan for their help on this project. Thanks also must be extended to Lizbeth Nauta whose incredible talent has strengthened this and so many other works produced or published by Combined Books. Other assistance with the *Atlanta Campaign* was rendered by Vince Perkins, Fan Fei Wan, Heidi Kidon, Colleen Brophy and Tom Maguire. Special mention must go to Susanna Spiers for her superlative wisdom, generosity and extraordinary magnanimity. Finally, I owe a special debt of gratitude to Gretchen Nielsen and Lizbeth Jablonski whose unparalleled scholarship, kindness and friendship provided untold inspiration for this volume.

Special thanks to the United States Army Historical Institute for allowing us to reproduce valuable photographs from their extensive collection.

Contents

Introduction	6
CHAPTER I: Johnston Takes Command	9
CHAPTER II: Building An Offensive	17
CHAPTER III: Rocky Face Ridge	33
CHAPTER IV: Resaca	43
CHAPTER V: Trap at Cassville	53
CHAPTER VI: Hell Hole	61
CHAPTER VII: Before the Three Mountain Line	75
CHAPTER VIII: Kennesaw Mountain	87
CHAPTER IX: To the Chattahoochee	101
CHAPTER X: Peachtree Creek	111
CHAPTER XI: The Battle of Atlanta	119
CHAPTER XII: Ezra Church	131
CHAPTER XIII: Utoy Creek to Jonesboro	141
CHAPTER XIV: "Atlanta is Ours and Fairly Won."	161
Bibliography	175

Introduction

Built in the mid-1800s, the Western & Atlantic Railroad wound its way southwest from Chattanooga, over the rugged terrain of north Georgia, southeast through sleepy towns, and across the pleasant brown waters of rolling rivers towards its destination, Atlanta, Georgia. By 1864, the Western & Atlantic had lost its idyllic charm and had become the highway of invasion for a Federal army led by a grim warrior, Major General William Tecumseh Sherman. Sherman's offensive into Georgia against the Army of Tennessee was played out for almost three months on the 120 miles of the railroad between Chattanooga and Atlanta, at places such as Rocky Face Ridge, Resaca, Kennesaw Mountain and Atlanta itself. Sherman later wrote of the line, "Every foot of it should be sacred ground, because it was moistened by patriotic blood." This long and sanguinary contest fought throughout northern and central Georgia became known as the Atlanta campaign.

When Sherman left East Tennessee to embark on his onslaught into Georgia, Atlanta was not the stated objective of the Federal general. Instead, his directives from his commander, Lieutenant General Ulysses S. Grant, called for the destruction of General Joseph E. Johnston's Army of Tennessee and the ruination of Confederate resources used to supply the Rebel armies in the field. However, Atlanta's importance to both armies made the city a target for Federal planners and an object of defense by Confederate strategists.

During the Civil War, Atlanta, Georgia and the surrounding area became increasingly vital to the survival of the Confederacy. Its industries provided Confederate armies in the field with small arms, artillery, ammunition and clothes, while its buildings served as command centers, storehouses and hospitals. The loss of the productive capacity of central Tennessee early in the war added to the critical importance of Atlanta's industrial and commercial potential to the Confederate war effort.

Atlanta was also a major hub of rail traffic. Four Confederate arteries converged here, the Georgia Railroad, the Atlanta & West Point Railroad, the Macon & Western Railroad and the Atlanta & Western Railroad, through which pulsed commerce as well as the supplies and reinforcements necessary for fighting armies. The lines linked the city with other vital points in the Confederacy. The Georgia Railroad ran west from the city through Rutledge, Augusta, and Charleston, South Carolina, and connected with the Confederate capital of Richmond, Virginia. The Atlantic & West Point veered off to the southwest to link Atlanta with Montgomery and the port city of Mobile, Alabama. To the south, ran the Macon & Western which led to Macon and Savannah. The Western & Atlantic headed north for Chattanooga. With these lines cut, the eastern states of the South would be severed from the rest of the Confederacy.

Though Sherman claimed in his memoirs, "Neither Atlanta, nor Augusta, nor Savannah, was his objective, but the 'army of Jos. Johnston'," Atlanta took on symbolic importance for the entire campaign into Georgia. Certainly Sherman was intent on crushing the Army of Tennessee which opposed him under General Joseph E. Johnston and later General John Bell Hood, but this objective could not be attained without the seizure and desolation of Atlanta. From May to September of 1864, Sherman applied himself almost single-mindedly to this task.

Insignia of the Atlanta campaign, lines of entrenchments. The combat during the struggle for Atlanta presaged the trench warfare of World War I.

8 / THE ATLANTA CAMPAIGN

Soldiers of the Army of the Cumberland *storm entrenched Southern positions on Missionary Ridge. The collapse of the Confederate Army of Tennessee in the battles outside Chattanooga on 24-25 November 1863 led to the replacement of the unit's commander, Braxton Bragg, with Joseph E. Johnston.*

CHAPTER I

JOHNSTON TAKES COMMAND

November, 1863 - April, 1864

During the closing months of 1863, the Confederacy was forced to confront a long festering crisis of command in the western theater of operations. It was on 24-25 November that the Army of Tennessee under General Braxton Bragg suffered a catastrophic military defeat at Chattanooga, Tennessee. On those fateful Autumn days, Federal attacks easily crumpled seemingly impregnable Confederate lines on the heights of Lookout Mountain and Missionary Ridge. Beaten, disorganized and demoralized, the remnants of the Army of Tennessee fell back 25 miles to the southeast to form a new defensive position near the town of Dalton in northwest Georgia. The battlefield failures at Chattanooga were to have a telling impact on the plight of the Confederacy; not only was the loyal Southern state of Tennessee lost to the Yankees, but, more importantly, the enemy had gained possession of a vital gateway to the lower South. Once a large Union army was martialed at Chattanooga, it would be poised to launch a destructive campaign against the Confederate industrial and agricultural resources in Georgia, Alabama and possibly other states, such as the Carolinas. If the South was to survive the war, something had to done. Confederate leaders searched in desperation for a means of salvaging the military situation in the West before the North could reap the advantages of its victory at Chattanooga and wreak further damage on the South.

In December of 1863, president of the Confederacy, Jefferson Davis, sought a suitable general to take command of the Army of Tennessee and reverse the tide of misfortune which had forced the army back to Dalton. Defeats, retreats, rancor among the commanders and low morale among the troops of the Army of Tennessee had forced Bragg to tender his resignation on 28 November. Nevertheless, the president continued to have a great deal of confidence in the North Carolinian and ordered him to Richmond to serve as his military adviser.

Davis faced difficult choices as he searched through a limited pool of talented and

Jefferson Davis, president of the Confederate States of America.

capable generals for the best successor to Bragg. At first the president looked to the ranks of the Army of Tennessee for a possible candidate. Specifically, the man Davis had in mind was Lieutenant General William J. Hardee who was in temporary command of the army in the wake of Bragg's departure. The author of a manual on field tactics used by both armies, Hardee was regarded as a solid fighting commander, known to the ranks as "Old Reliable." However, the general was not interested in the promotion and balked at the idea of taking on the greater responsibilities of army command.

Davis' other possibilities were Generals Joseph E. Johnston, Pierre Gustav Toutant Beauregard and the commander of the Army of Northern Virginia, General Robert E. Lee. Davis had reason to be dissatisfied with Virginian Johnston and the Creole Beauregard since both men had commanded Confederate armies before and, in his opinion, not at all satisfactorily. Furthermore, both, especially Johnston, had reputations for quarreling frequently with the president and were known to be allied with some of Davis' political enemies. Little wonder, then, that Davis chose to look elsewhere before appointing one of these men.

The "Gray Fox," General Robert E. Lee, seemed to be Davis' best choice for the post. Indeed, there was no better general in all the Confederacy. The president decided to consult with Lee in early December about the possibility of his assuming command of the Army of Tennessee. However, Lee was unenthusiastic about any transfer from his beloved Army of Northern Virginia. Rather than acquiesce to the president's desires, Lee pointed to numerous difficulties which would be posed by his relocation west. With extreme politeness he complained that he would probably not be able to win from the Western generals the "cordial" cooperation needed to win victories. Furthermore, the government would again be faced with the quandary of finding a suitable candidate for army command, for the Army the Northern Virginia. Instead, Lee briefly suggested Beauregard for the post at Dalton.

On 9 December, Lee was called to Richmond to confer over the selection of a successor to Bragg with Davis and Secretary of War James A. Seddon. Lee fully expected that he would be transferred west, despite his objections. Before he left for the capital he confided this belief to his cavalry commander, J. E. B. Stuart, in a solemn note. "I am called to Richmond this morning by the president," he wrote. "I presume the rest will follow. My heart and thoughts will always be with this army."

The conference lasted for over a week and its result was to provoke controversy for many years to come. Overcoming his manifold reservations about the general, Davis decided to place Joseph E. Johnston in command of the force at Dalton.

Johnston was considered an able general by military men on both sides. His résumé of field experience included service in the Battle of Bull Run, the defence of Richmond against Major General George B. McClellan's Army of the Potomac and a theater command in the west during the Vicksburg and Stone's River campaigns. Though his record was hardly stunning, his reputation was almost unexcelled by any other general save the superlative Lee.

Despite Johnston's prestige, his appointment contained much risk. Davis and Johnston harbored an almost incurable animosity for one another which supposedly stemmed from their days at West Point. Evidently their common cause in fighting the war for Southern independence did little to heal this antipathy. Throughout the conflict, both men engaged in numerous spats that had so far only proved detrimental to the war effort. Johnston's service under the president led to the general's cultivation of an almost paranoid belief that Davis was intent on seeing him fail, and his career in ruins. At the same time, Davis was consistently unsupportive of Johnston during his various commands and unfairly blamed him for such setbacks as the capitulation of Vicksburg. Moreover, the Confederate president became irritated by Johnston's penchant of avoiding battle, and was insulted by his frequent failure or refusal to keep Richmond properly informed of his plans. Despite their ever growing dislike for one another, both were willing to work together for the time being; Davis felt Johnston was the right man to win a major victory in the West and Johnston was eager for another chance at army command.

Soon after Johnston arrived in Dalton on 27 December, the general and the president, true to form, began to argue, this time about the viability of launching an offensive in early 1864. Both Davis and his military adviser, Braxton Bragg, encouraged by erroneous positive reports of the Army of Tennessee's condition from Hardee, were of the opinion that the unit was in good enough shape to invade Tennessee and engage Federal forces there. Furthermore, the time was ripe for an attack. The Confederates were receiving indications that the enemy was drawing significant forces from the West in order to launch another powerful "On to Richmond" campaign in Virginia. Thus, a strong Army of Tennessee should be able to make some headway against the weakened National forces which remained in Tennessee. Johnston, however, had reason to feel differently.

When the general arrived at Dalton, he found an army which only faintly resembled the one described by sources in Richmond. The Army of Tennessee was hardly in fighting shape, but was instead in a desperate condition. The troops lacked important supplies such as small arms, food, blankets and shoes. Johnston remarked that the number of barefoot troops was "painful to see." Moreover, cavalry and artillery horses were weak from lack of forage and could not perform the tasks required of them. Worse still, the morale of the army was dreadfully low; desertions had depleted Confederate rolls while sickness, drinking and gambling were prevalent amongst the men who remained. An inadequate supply system forestalled any improvements to the disheartening situation and any attempts to inaugurate an early offensive.

Joseph E. Johnston
1807-1891

Joseph Eggleston Johnston, perhaps the most enigmatic military figure of the Civil War, hailed from Virginia and graduated from West Point in 1829, a classmate of Robert E. Lee. His pre-Civil War military career was to be varied and one of the most distinguished of his fellow Confederate officers. Johnston saw action in the Black Hawk War and the Second Seminole War and a year of civil engineering work in Florida. During the Mexican War, he was employed on Winfield Scott's staff and led a storming column against Chapultepec in Mexico City. After the war, he served as chief of topographical engineers in Texas, commanded a cavalry regiment on the frontier, and served as a staff officer in the Utah Expedition against the Mormons. By the time of the Civil War, he was a brigadier general and quartermaster general of the army.

Johnston resigned his commission five days after Fort Sumter, when Virginia left the Union. His potential was immediately recognized and he was commissioned as a major general in the service of his native state. Soon after this appointment, Johnston was given the rank of brigadier general in the Confederate Regular Army and took command at Harper's Ferry, where one of his subordinates was the soon-to-be-eminent Thomas Jonathan Jackson.

Though engaged at First Bull Run, Johnston let Brigadier General Pierre Toutant Beauregard command the Rebel army during the battle while he took a supplemental role. After the battle, Johnston was promoted to the rank of full general in the Confederate army. However, the new general was insulted to find himself ranked merely fourth amongst the five full generals of the Confederacy. He then proceeded to open a testy argument with President Jefferson Davis over the matter further fuelling a pre-existing animosity between them.

During the fall and winter of 1861-1862, Johnston set about building what would become the elite fighting force known as the Army of Northern Virginia. He led this command in a defense against Major General George Brinton McClellan's *Army of the Potomac* during the Peninsular campaign of March-June 1862. Though Johnston allowed the enemy to move within almost seven miles of the Confederate capital of Richmond, he struck him at the battle of Seven Pines, on 1 June 1862. The general suffered severe wounds during the engagement and was forced to relinquish his command to Robert E. Lee.

Johnston convalesced for some time before he returned to an active command. In November of 1862, he was placed in charge of the Department of the West, which oversaw the actions of Lieutenant General John C. Pemberton's army at Vicksburg and the Army of Tennessee under General Braxton Bragg in eastern Tennessee. Rather than diligently apply himself to the difficult tasks that he faced, Johnston sulked because his mission was ambiguous and he was not given full authority over both forces. Worse still, he quarreled with the petulant Davis over strategy. During Johnston's tenure in this post, the Confederacy suffered major reverses, such as Stone's River and the loss of Vicksburg. Davis blamed Johnston for many of the setbacks in the West, especially the capitulation of Vicksburg, and later relieved Johnston from theater command.

Despite the ill-will between the president and Johnston, the general was placed in a position of great responsibility in December of 1863, as the head of the Army of Tennessee. Over the winter and spring of 1864, he continued to quarrel with Davis, this time about the viability of undertaking an offensive with the Army of Tennessee. Before the Confederates finally got around to planning a possible advance, Major General William T. Sherman beat them to the punch; he was on the move from Chattanooga in

---

After taking stock of the army's condition at Dalton, Johnston replied to Richmond's calls to move north by declaring that his army would not be able to advance for some time. Instead of going on the attack, Johnston preferred to wait at Dalton, improve the state of his forces, allow the Federals to advance, defeat them and then pursue the retreating enemy into Tennessee. Such a passive strategy was not likely to impress or enthuse the authorities in Richmond.

Indeed, Davis was hardly content with this policy and in March of 1864, he pressured Johnston to accept a proposal to take the offensive in a daring move meant to throw the Federals off balance and force them back into the interior of Tennessee. The ambitious plan which Davis and Bragg had in mind called for a combined advance of the Army of Tennessee and Lieutenant General James Longstreet's Corps

Two of the greatest leaders of the Confederacy, Joseph E. Johnston (at left) and Robert E. Lee (at right).

May 1864. Johnston's command and planning during the campaign from May to 17 July remains controversial to this day. Some see his retreat south before Sherman as a set of strategic masterpieces which stymied his enemy. Critics find the general guilty of incompetence, and question whether he actually had a plan to counter his foe. Whatever the truth, Davis became dissatisfied with the results of Johnston's command and replaced him on 17 July 1864 with the more belligerent John Bell Hood.

Though Johnston remained inactive for several months after his relief, in February, 1865 newly appointed general in chief Robert E. Lee returned him to command of the Army of Tennessee. Johnston led the now paltry force against his old enemy Sherman during the closing months of the war. Shortly after Appomattox, on 18 April 1865, Davis surrendered his troops to Sherman.

After the great conflict, Johnston's career blossomed in more peaceful enterprises. He enjoyed some success in the insurance business, served as a congressman from Virginia, 1879-1881, became a national commissioner of railroads, and enjoyed friendships with his former enemies, Sherman and Grant. At Sherman's funeral in February of 1891, Johnston bared his head in honor of his former adversary despite cold weather and a driving rain. He caught pneumonia by this noble act and died a month later.

---

of the Army of Northern Virginia which had spent the winter months of 1863-1864 in East Tennessee. Johnston was to sidestep the Union army at Chattanooga, join up with Longstreet, and then press on to Nashville, drawing the enemy along with them. Unfortunately, the plan was all too daring for a general who was not known for taking chances and gambling with the fate of his troops.

Johnston rejected such grandiose maneuvers out of hand as his army was hardly capable of undertaking such a risky venture in early 1864. Instead he offered a less vigorous scheme of his own, which called for part of his army to advance on the Federal line of communications with Knoxville, Tennessee. This action would supposedly draw the Federals out of Chattanooga for a fight on Confederate terms. Though Johnston was giving in to Davis' demands to take to the offensive, the

Confederate Emancipation

As the year 1864 dawned, the future of the Confederacy appeared to be bleak. Drastic measures were needed to win major victories. On 2 January, Major General Patrick R. Cleburne, a divisional commander in the Army of Tennessee, suggested a policy to save the Confederacy which was almost totally antithetical to Southern ideals: the emancipation of slaves. The idea was drastic and revolutionary, but Cleburne believed emancipation might prove to be the salvation of his beleaguered nation.

After almost three years of war, Confederate ranks had been substantially depleted through combat deaths and injuries, capture, disease, desertion and various other causes. Lacking the North's immense reserves of manpower, the South had a limited reservoir of potential soldiers from which to strengthen its armies in the field. Cleburne believed that the answer was to free black slaves, train them as soldiers and have them take to the field to fight against their supposed liberators. While emancipation appeared an extreme solution, Cleburne was convinced of its benefits; not only would the recruitment of slaves stem the tide of blacks joining the Union forces, but it might even win European recognition of the South. Acknowledging that the idea might be unpopular, Cleburne offered his services to train and command a black regiment.

In late 1863, Cleburne drafted a proposal and showed it to the officers of the division. Cleburne's subordinates warned their commander against making his plan public, as it would ruin the general's chances for promotion and possibly even destroy his career. Still, his entire brigade and 10 regimental commanders gave their support by signing the document.

On 2 January, Cleburne met division and corps commanders of the Army of Tennessee at Johnston's headquarters to put forward his plan. Though he managed to enlist the support of several fellow generals, such as Major General Benjamin F. Cheatham, Major General Thomas C. Hindman and Brigadier General John Kelly, the outraged opponents were vociferous in their disapproval. The most irate was Major General W. H. T. Walker, who went as far as to label the plan traitorous. While Johnston sought to quell potential discord in his command by tabling the issue, Walker was intent o bringing the matter to the attention of Jefferson Davis.

Walker was able to get a copy of the proposal from Cleburne and sent it off to Richmond with a list of the officers who supported it. Johnston was against making an issue out Cleburne's plan, deeming it a non-military matter, but Walker remained adamant. On 12 January he wrote the army commander,.

> The gravity of the subject, the magnitude of the issues involved, and my strong convictions that further agitation of such sentiments and propositions would ruin the efficiency of our army and involve our cause in ruin and disgrace, constitute my reason for bringing the document before the Executive.

A shocked Davis learned of the measure from Walker on 23 January. He later replied:

> Deeming it to be injurious to the public service that such a subject should be mooted or even known to be entertained by persons possessed of such confidence and respect of the people, I have concluded that the best policy under the circumstances will be to avoid all publicity, and the Secretary of War has therefore written to General Johnston requesting him to convey to those concerned my desire that it should be kept quiet. If it be kept out of the public journals its effect will be lessened.

Knowledge of Cleburne's proposal was effectively suppressed, but its impact had a more lasting effect. The idea had discredited the general in Richmond and obstructed any chance of his advancement to higher levels of command. Despite the disservice of his government, Cleburne continued to fight for the Confederacy and died for the cause on the battlefield of Franklin, Tennessee on 30 November. Ironically, the South began to create units of black soldiers late in the war, but the Confederacy surrendered before these troops could ever tested in the field.

---

president was decidedly unimpressed by the gesture.

Throughout the month of March and most of April, Johnston continued to quarrel with Davis and Bragg about the nature of a possible offensive. As their fight continued, the Army of Tennessee remained passively immobile while the unhindered Federals built up a powerful army at Chattanooga.

While Johnston's Army of Tennessee remained at Dalton however, the commanding general was successful in restoring the force to fighting shape. Johnston improved the logistical system so that his troops could be properly armed, fed and clothed. He

The Fort Pillow Massacre

One of the greatest controversies of the Civil War is the alleged massacre of Federal troops that occurred at Fort Pillow on 12 April 1864. On that fateful day, Confederate troopers under Nathan Bedford Forrest assaulted the earthen fortification situated on the Mississippi River 40 miles north of Nashville. Reports from survivors detail the horrific murder of soldiers after they had surrendered and given up their arms.

In April of 1864, Fort Pillow was occupied by 262 Afro-American troops of the *11th U.S. Colored Infantry* and *Battery F* of the *4th U.S. Colored Light Artillery*, as well as 295 troops of the *13th Tennessee (USA)* cavalry regiment. The garrison was under the command of a Major Lionel F. Booth. Lying in the waters next to the fort was the gun boat *New Era*.

At 0530 on 12 April, the fort came under attack from Confederate cavalry troopers. The first attack was composed of 1,500 men under Brigadier General James R. Chalmers. The Rebels enjoyed early success, managing to gain a piece of high ground near the fort which allowed them to send rifle fire into the interior of the enemy works. Major Booth was killed by enemy fire around 0900, and command fell to Major William F. Bradford.

As the day of battle progressed, the Confederates continued to post gains. By 1000, Forrest himself was on the scene to command the assault. An hour later, the Confederates managed to capture the barracks at the south end of the work and put a commanding fire into the fort. The guns of the *New Era* attempted to pound away at the enemy assailing Fort Pillow's garrison, but its fire had little or no effect. At 1300, the ship abandoned the garrison to its fate and sailed down river to replenish its stock of ammunition.

By 1530, the Confederates were in a position to demand surrender. Major Bradford asked for an hour to ponder the demand, but Forrest would grant him only 20 minutes to abandon the fort and surrender. Since a steamship loaded with reinforcements was seen bearing down on the fort, the Federals appeared to be stalling until help could arrive.

Forrest renewed his demands for a surrender, but Bradford refused. Forrest then launched an attack which drove the Federals from their works, back towards the river and into the sights of a Confederate force which was waiting for them. The surviving garrison troops then attempted to surrender, and this is when the controversy began.

According to Federal survivors, shouts went up from the Rebel ranks, such as "No quarter!" and "Kill the damned niggers; shoot them down!" Forrest's command then proceeded to engage in horrendous acts of butchery, killing men, women and children as well as the sick and wounded. Bodies were hacked apart with sabres, and some Confederates scalped their enemies. Some Federals were lined up and shot, and their corpses were then thrown into the river. Forrest's troops reportedly even set fire to huts containing wounded soldiers who were to weak to crawl to safety. Once the Rebels had finished their handiwork, they threw the dead and even some of the living, into a trench and buried them.

For their part, the Confederates claimed there was no massacre during the battle. Some Federal soldiers were shot evidently "trying to escape," or for picking up their guns and firing on the Southerners after they had supposedly surrendered, but no wholesale slaughter, as the Yankees described.

The number of casualties confirm that the Confederates handled the garrison in a harsher manner than was necessary. Around 230 Federals were killed, an abnormally large figure for a battle of this kind, 100 were wounded and 226 men were captured. The Confederates murdered captured black soldiers on numerous occasions during the war and probably resorted to acts of barbarism at Fort Pillow. There was also severe antipathy against fellow Southerners from Tennessee who had cast their lot with the Union. Regardless of the reasons, Fort Pillow serves as a cruel reminder that the Civil War was a bitter and cruel struggle, and not the genteel conflict described by certain Romanticists.

The Federal command of Afro American and White Troops at Fort, Pillow, Tennessee is massacred after they surrendered to Confederate troops under Nathan Bedford Forrest. Some 230 Federals were killed out of a garrison of around 560 men in the battle and massacre at Fort Pillow.

also sponsored efforts to win back deserters with an amnesty policy, and improved the morale of many veterans by granting furloughs. Drills, training and even unit snowball fights were employed to revive the army's determination and sense of pride for the real battles to come. By April, Johnston's acts had won him the support of the troops of the Army of Tennessee who quickly became confident they were now in the hands of a general who would eventually lead them to victory.

When Johnston finally did engage in battle, he would initially wield 55,000 men in two corps, one led by Hardee and the other in the charge of a transfer from the Army of Northern Virginia, Lieutenant General John Bell Hood. Hood came west with a deservedly splendid reputation as a hard fighter, earned by fighting in most of the major battles in the east and at Chickamauga. While Johnston looked upon this addition to the army as a potential boon, the general's ambition and aversion for Johnston's Fabian ways of war only served to undermine the commander of the Army of Tennessee. Throughout the coming campaign, Hood would back stab Johnston by sending secret reports to Richmond maligning that general's ability and judgement. Davis did not need another reason to lack faith in Johnston, but Hood's surreptitious reports gave him grist to his mill.

Though a revitalized Army of Tennessee stood ready at Dalton during the spring months of 1864, certain command problems still existed within the leadership of the force which were already hindering any chance of success. Davis' and Johnston's incessant quarreling failed to accomplish much of anything other than giving the Federals the opportunity to move against the Army of Tennessee at their leisure. This mutual lack of confidence would debilitate the war effort in other ways as well. Johnston didn't demand much reason to move with extreme caution, but Davis' demonstrated distrust would further ensure his refusal to risk attacks in the coming campaign. However, the general maintained the faith of his men, which was ultimately what he would need most to defeat the enemy once his legions descended on Dalton from East Tennessee.

CHAPTER II

BUILDING AN OFFENSIVE

March - May, 1864

After the victories at Chattanooga, Major General Ulysses S. Grant, the commander of the Federal Western theater, and his favorite subordinate, Major General William Tecumseh Sherman, contemplated the destruction of the Army of Tennessee and an invasion into the interior of Georgia to destroy the Confederate resources in Atlanta. In March, when Grant left for Washington to assume the post of general in chief and Sherman took his place as commander of the West, these plans solidified into what would eventually become the Atlanta campaign.

Newly promoted Lieutenant General Grant hoped to launch at least two simultaneous movements into Georgia by the beginning of May while he remained in Virginia to oversee a drive against the Army of Northern Virginia. One prong of the offensive would be under Sherman, advancing south from Chattanooga towards Atlanta. On 4 April, Grant sent a dispatch to Sherman detailing the objectives set for his subordinate, "You I propose to move against Johnston's army, to break it up, and to get into the interior of the enemy's country as far as you can, inflicting all the damage you can against their war resources." As to the actual shape of Sherman's advance Grant wrote, "I do not propose to lay down for you a plan of campaign, but simply to lay down the work it is desirable to have done, and leave you free to execute it in your own way." Sherman's advance would be complemented by another offensive, under Major General Nathaniel P. Banks. Banks was to take the port city of Mobile, Alabama, and hence advance northeast into Georgia. While these moves were under way, Grant would ensure that the Confederate armies in the East and West would be so occupied that they would not be able to maintain or strengthen each other. As Sherman and Banks advanced through Georgia, and Grant directed the Federal offensive against Richmond, all assaults would work to block any cooperation or reinforcement between Lee and Johnston. Grant and Sherman, in formulating their offensives of 1864 into Virginia and Georgia, had developed a brilliant strategy;

18 / THE ATLANTA CAMPAIGN

President Abraham Lincoln bestows Ulysses S. Grant with his commission as lieutenant general. Grant was the first officer to hold the prestigious rank since George Washington.

after years of wasted motion, the massive Northern superiority in men and material would finally be properly utilized by simultaneous offensives to attack and wear down the enemy's resources.

By April, Sherman had inspected his forces and was aware of the immense difficulties he would face in launching an offensive that Spring. Overall, Sherman's primary problem was logistical. A continuous supply of vast resources was essential to support his army when it took to the offensive in hostile territory and over difficult terrain. Due to the lack of navigable rivers in East Tennessee and on the path of Sherman's advance, the availability of supplies would be totally dependent on rail transportation. Thus, the Federals would have to count on the railroad from Louisville to Nashville and Chattanooga as well as the Western & Atlantic line for 120 miles as they descended into Georgia for Atlanta.

Sherman's reliance on the railroads could prove to be his Achilles heel. If the Confederates were able to get a cavalry or infantry force in the Federal rear and destroy the railroad at any time, Sherman's army might find itself cut off from supplies and forced to abandon the campaign. Furthermore, troops detailed for the necessary protection of the railroad only served to make Sherman's army weaker when he needed all it's strength to confront Confederate forces in Georgia. This problem would inevitably be augmented as more troops were detached to protect the increasingly tenuous supply line as Sherman moved farther south.

As a solution to such difficulties, Sherman sought to build a massive stockpile of supplies which could sustain his army throughout the future campaign and would obviate reliance on the lengthy supply line from the North. Sherman's objective was

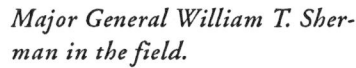

Major General William T. Sherman in the field.

to amass 70 days' supplies for approximately 100,000 men sufficient to enable them to launch an offensive. With such a supply on hand and close by, Sherman could afford to wait, fight or advance if his lines were ever cut.

Sherman reduced his dependence on the long rail route extending from Louisville, Kentucky by making Nashville his main supply depot and Chattanooga, his forward base. To build his reservoir of supplies, vast amounts of weaponry, ammunition, food and other articles were collected at Nashville and funneled to the Federal forces massing near Chattanooga. The accomplishment of this task proved fraught with much difficulty since the railroad from Nashville to Chattanooga only barely had sufficient capacity to supply Federal forces in East Tennessee, let alone support any advance deep into Georgia.

Sherman was forced to desperate measures to solve his predicament. On 6 April, the general limited all rail traffic in East Tennessee to military purposes. All civilian travel and cargo was forbidden in favor of essential military shipments of food, ammunition and other supplies. To make room on the trains, troops were required to march towards Chattanooga, beef cattle were herded to the front and all garrisons within 30 miles of Nashville were to receive their supplies by wagon. Sherman's

Atlanta

A street of shops in Atlanta, Georgia including an auction house dealing in slaves.

The city of Atlanta, which was to attain such great importance during the Civil War, was the direct product of railroad building in Georgia. The town grew up after the General Assembly of Georgia, passed an act creating the Western & Atlantic Railroad. The line was to link the Tennessee River Valley with the interior of Georgia where it would connect with branch lines heading to the coast and other states. The point where the lines would meet was set on the high ground, a few miles south of the Chattahoochee. Lieutenant Colonel Stephen Harriman was detailed to survey the appointed area to find an appropriate site to link the Western & Atlantic with branch lines. Beginning his task on 4 July 1837, Harriman finally picked a place six and one half miles to the southeast of the Chattahoochee River in November of that year.

Three years later, the engineers of the lines picked the exact point where the railroads would meet and a town would be built. They gave the location the apt, if unaspiring name of Terminus. Over the next few years, trains came rolling through, and though speculation was rampant, the town grew sluggishy. In

measures prompted a great public outcry which forced President Abraham Lincoln to investigate the general's unpopular action. However, the president was immediately placated when Sherman explained the exigencies behind his important campaign.

Still, Sherman's draconian railroad policy was not enough to build the necessary stockpile at Chattanooga due to a lack of rolling stock. He next decided to seize all locomotives and cars arriving at Nashville from Louisville to service his army's needs. The president of the Louisville & Nashville Railroad complained, but Sherman

Building An Offensive / 21

What made Atlanta one of the South's greatest cities as well as a target for Northern military leaders, railroads. Atlanta was the junction of four major lines the Western & Atlantic Railroad, the Georgia Railroad, the Macon & Western Railroad and the Atlanta and West Point Railroad.

1843, its name was changed to Marthasville in honor of Governor Wilson Lumpkin's daughter. By the mid-1840s, the town was growing robustly and needed a new name with a more attractive and impressive sound and feeling. For this, Atlanta, the feminine form of the Latin word for Atlantic, was chosen.

By 1850, the city of Atlanta was beginning to hum with growth and prosperity. The city had finally been linked by rail with Chattanooga and Savannah and was becoming a major center of American commerce. The decade before the Civil War brought more settlers who started industries, opened a variety of stores and built new homes. In 1848, the town only contained about 3,000 people. Twelve years later, 11,572 people made their homes there. The vibrancy of the city and the confidence of its citizens led to the creation of a movement to make Atlanta the state capital.

When Georgia seceded, the citizens of Atlanta cheered the birth of the newborn Confederacy. Little did they know that in three years they would be subject to one of the greatest military campaigns in history, live in fear under a bombardment of Federal guns, and see all that they had built burned to the ground in a few short days.

"appealed to his patriotism" and even convinced him to appropriate all the rolling stock coming south into Jeffersonville, Indiana. Sherman later wrote of the spectacle created by his efforts during his famous campaign into Georgia, ."..in a short time we had cars and locomotives from almost every road at the North; months afterward I was amused to see, away down in Georgia, cars marked 'Pittsburg & Fort Wayne', 'Delaware & Lackawana', 'Baltimore & Ohio', and indeed with the names of almost every railroad north of the Ohio River."

William T. Sherman
1820-1891

Ohioan William Tecumseh Sherman was one of eleven children born to attorney and judge Charles R. Sherman and his wife, Mary Hoyt Sherman. Sherman was aptly named Tecumseh, or "shooting star," after the famous Shawnee Indian chief and warrior. Nicknamed "Cump" by his relatives, Sherman was baptized as William in 1829.

The death of Sherman's father in 1829 led to a separation from his brothers and sisters who were distributed amongst various family members for care and education. Sherman himself was taken in by the family of Senator Thomas Ewing of Ohio.

Sherman entered an artillery regiment as second lieutenant after graduating sixth in West Point's class of 1840. While his compatriots saw combat in various campaigns, Sherman's term in the military involved uneventful periods of service in Florida, Alabama, Georgia, South Carolina and California. After 13 years in the army, he resigned and engaged in a series of civilian pursuits. Nothing in

Major General William T. Sherman

Sherman's activities before the Civil War heralded the strategic mastermind who would wage war with such intensity and determination. He ran a bank in California until it failed in 1857. After this unsuccessful venture, Sherman headed east to Kansas to take up law, but only proved moderately talented in his father's profession. He then applied for and received the presidency of the Louisiana State Seminary and Military Academy (today's Louisiana State University), in October of 1859. When Louisiana seceded in 1861, Sherman took his family north to St. Louis, to become president of a street car company. When war finally broke out, Sherman joined the Union forces as a colonel in the *13th Infantry* of the Regular Army and was later appointed to brigade command in Brigadier General David Tyler's *First Division*. Sherman led the unit at the disastrous battle of Bull Run, where it suffered the heaviest losses of all the Union brigades involved. His meritorious service was rewarded with a brigadier generalcy on 7 August.

Having been transferred west to serve in Major General Robert Anderson's Department of the Cumberland in the fall of 1862, Sherman received full command

---

At the same time, Sherman took measures to provide adequate protection for his rail network. Thousands of militia troops were mustered into "100-day regiments" to guard the railway in Kentucky and Tennessee, while closer to the front Sherman would rely on veteran troops. Some of these troops were detailed in block houses near vital positions such as tunnels and trestles. Repair facilities located at these positions allowed a hasty mending of any serious damage incurred by the Confederates. Mounted strikes were also launched into Alabama and Mississippi to keep Rebel raiders occupied and away from the railway in Kentucky, Tennessee and Georgia. With his logistical difficulties addressed, Sherman could be confident that his army would be ready to move by May.

During the month of April, Federal strategy was to undergo a discouraging modification. Before Banks assisted Sherman in the campaign into Georgia, he had embarked on an advance up the Red River against Shreveport, Louisiana to further destabilize the Confederacy of the Trans-Mississippi, free up Federal troops protecting commerce on the Mississippi River, and allow cotton from Louisiana to be shipped to Northern mills. Sherman transferred 10,000 of his own troops to assist in

of the post when Anderson fell ill. The experience proved injurious to Sherman's reputation as the general grew incredibly tense and flustered under the responsibility and fought with newspaper reporters, who retaliated by writing that general was losing his mind. These rumors of Sherman's mental breakdown led to his removal, but fortunately the general found employment as the leader of the *Fifth Division* in Major General Ulysses S. Grant's *Army of the Tennessee*. Sherman was almost ruined when his division was surprised on the first day of Shiloh, 6 April 1862, but his hard fighting helped to save the day and his reputation from further disaster.

After Shiloh, Sherman was appointed major general, and his fortunes steadily improved along with those of his commander Grant. Throughout 1862-1863, Sherman campaigned in the Mississippi Valley in Grant's famous attempts to take Vicksburg. He suffered defeat at Chickasaw Bluffs in December 1862, but won a substantial victory at Arkansas Post a month later, and led the *XV Corps* in the great victories of Grant's Vicksburg campaign.

When Grant was appointed to command the Military Division of the Mississippi, Sherman took that generals old command of the *Army of the Tennessee*, which he led at Missionary Ridge on 25 November. Grant's promotion to command of all the U.S. armies led to Sherman's appointment to the Military Division of the Mississippi and control of all the Federal forces in the western theater. In May, he launched his famous Atlanta campaign, which culminated in the capture of that city after four months of heavy fighting. Sherman then advanced from Atlanta to the port city of Savannah, with the intention of making Georgia "howl" along the way. Sherman's troops, called "bummers," effectively tore apart the countryside with emotionless deliberation during the advance. Their depredations have since become the stuff of infamous legend. After taking the port town, Sherman advanced north into the Carolinas, where he forced General Joseph E. Johnston to surrender on 18 April 1865.

After the war, Sherman continued in the army, first as a lieutenant general in 1866, and then as a full general and commanding general of the army after Grant was elected president, in 1868. During his stormy tenure commanding general, Sherman prosecuted destructive wars against the Indians and created the Command and General Staff College at Fort Leavenworth. After Sherman retired in 1883, he received requests to run for the presidency, to which he responded "If nominated I will not run, if elected, I will not serve." He died in New York City eight years later.

Sherman remains one of the greatest military strategists in American history. His development of a modern approach to war, which involved the destruction of enemy resources as well as extensive depredations to weary the Confederate populace, have since become fundamentals of contemporary warfare.

Banks' Red River operation, confident that they would be returned by the time the campaign into Georgia was underway in May. However, Banks' campaign was an atrocious fiasco and despite an overwhelming advantage in numbers, his marginal military abilities precipitated an incredible defeat at Sabine's Crossroads by Major General Richard B. Taylor's Confederate army on 8-9 April. Given the setback of the Red River Campaign, Grant was forced to concede that Banks' troops would be unavailable for any assault against Mobile. Sherman would have to drive back Johnston's army on his own. Worse still, the 10,000 men Sherman had lent Banks wouldn't return to his army for the coming campaign either.

Though Sherman's army was depleted and its task complicated by the Red River fiasco, he still maintained a large force of seasoned troops led by capable generals. His command was divided into three armies: the *Army of the Cumberland*, the *Army of the Tennessee* and the *Army of the Ohio*. The largest contingent was the *Army of the Cumberland*, some 75,000 men strong, under the capable leadership of Major General George Henry Thomas. This force was composed primarily of western veterans who had fought at Perryville, Chickamauga and Missionary Ridge, and also included the

Women of the South compelled to appeal to a Federal commissary for food. The ravages of war on East Tennessee forced many citizens to rely on the Union armies as a source for food.

XX Corps, an amalgam of the *XI* and *XII* corps sent from the *Army of the Potomac* to break the Confederate siege of Chattanooga. The imperturbable commander of the *Army of the Cumberland* was a Virginian loyal to the Union whose main claim to fame was his stalwart defense at Chickamauga.

The *Army of the Tennessee* was Grant's and Sherman's old command which had seen service at Vicksburg and Chattanooga. At the beginning of the Atlanta campaign, the army's ranks were somewhat depleted. One division of the *XVI Corps* was detailed to the Mississippi valley and the entire *XVII Corps* was still on veteran furlough,

The Meridian Raid

By the winter of 1863-1864, the Federals were poised to launch a daring series of attacks which would extinguish the short life of the Confederacy and finally reunite the United States. The National armies had the manpower, the supplies and the generals to accomplish this task, but they still faced severe difficulties which could easily deny success. As the Federal armies advanced deep into enemy territory, they would be operating off of vulnerable exterior lines of supply that could easily be cut, forcing an army to retreat or attack on disadvantageous grounds. Furthermore, if the Federals successfully managed to advance into the South, their armies would become dangerously dispersed as troops were detached to defend and hold territory taken along the way. Thus, while the Federal armies were diffusing, the Rebels could concentrate and fall upon the weakened and exposed force at their leisure. With these concerns in mind, any advance into the heart of the Confederacy would be fraught with peril.

However, Lieutenant General Ulysses S. Grant and Major General William T. Sherman devised a method to obviate such Federal weaknesses and potential Confederate advantages. The strategy which they eventually employed was the use of destructive raids. Raids were movements into enemy territory, not to hold ground but to lay waste to the enemy's land and resources and deprive him of the ability to wage war effectively. By destroying civilian as well as military targets, the raid could also dissipate popular support for the continuance of the conflict. Since the objective of the raid was not to occupy territory, the force in question could advance to almost any point without supply lines, by living off the land. Grant and Sherman put this strategy to the test in early 1864 with the Meridian raid.

During February of 1864, Sherman launched a destructive raid from Vicksburg, across Mississippi, to the town of Meridian, the junction of a rail line between Vicksburg and Montgomery and the Mobile & Ohio Railroad. The move would have numerous important effects: it would destroy vital railroads, deprive the Confederates of the ability to draw supplies from Mississippi, clear that section of enemy troops, stop the Confederate "molestation" of river boats cruising along the Mississippi River, and protect Memphis and Nashville from any major Confederate attacks. The entire action would effectively reduce any Confederate threat from Mississippi and free up Federal troops for assaults on Atlanta and Mobile.

A long column of Federals winds it way through the Mississippi countryside on its way to Meridian, Mississippi. For the most part, Sherman's raid against the city of Meridian encountered hardly any Confederate opposition.

Sherman's attack was originally to take the form of an advance of 20,000 men, divided into two columns under Major General James B. McPherson and Major General S. A. Hurlbut, upon Meridian from Vicksburg. While the main advance was under way, land and naval forces in Mississippi, Louisiana and Tennessee would engage in feints and diversionary attacks to keep the Confederates off balance: Thomas would occupy Johnston and the Army of Tennessee with a demonstration before their position near Dalton; Schofield would be employed to a similar detail in East Tennessee, attracting the attention of James Longstreet's Corp, which had still not returned east to rejoin the Army of Northern Virginia; and the navy would provide a feint against the port city of Mobile, Alabama. At the same time, 7,000 cavalry troopers under Brigadier General Sooy Smith would advance on Meridian from Memphis to occupy and possibly destroy Nathan Bedford Forrest's cavalry, keeping that force from interfering with Sherman's campaign. Forrest's cavalry had been a constant irritant, threatening and destroying Federal communications in Tennessee. His downfall would be essential for any future campaign into Georgia. All this activity would use Federal manpower to circumvent Confederate superiority of interior lines and deprive the Rebels of the ability to concentrate against Sherman's forces.

On 3 February, Sherman started the 150-mile trek across Mississippi for Meridian with 35,000 soldiers. His troops passed through Brandon, Morton and Decatur without encountering any substantial opposition. On the way, the Federals engaged in the wholesale destruction of public and private property. Some were not totally unsympathetic. One Federal wrote, "I do not approve of the indiscriminate destruction and its horror can only be realized by witnessing them."

On the way to the Meridian, Sherman was once almost captured by a sudden cavalry attack near where he was bedding down for the night. The general quickly organized a motley group of clerks and orderlies to make a stand against the enemy, but fortunately an infantry force arrived before this "command" could be tested by a Confederate attack.

Sherman's immediate opposition in Mississippi was two divisions of infantry and two of cavalry under the Confederate "Fighting Bishop," Leonidas Polk, who had been transferred to departmental command of the Mississippi, Alabama and Louisiana in October of 1863. Polk was completely paralyzed by Sherman's advance. With only 9,000 troops, there was little he could do except avoid battle and call for reinforcements. Richmond pressed Johnston for help, but the commander of the Army of Tennessee had problems of his own when Thomas moved into his front to feign an attack. The inability of the Confederates to do much of anything to stop Sherman caused one Confederate to lament:

> It is a shame!—a stigma on the fair name of the Confederacy that thirty-five thousand hostile men should march entirely through Miss...and no obstacle be placed in the way to impede progress! We are told that the Country is devastated where they go,—That their trail is marked by the smoldering ruins of burned dwellings,—that crops are destroyed, and that life is laid waste by a remorseless foe.

Thus the Confederates were unable to act as Sherman's men took and systematically destroyed Meridian.

On 14 February the Federals triumphantly entered Meridian, Mississippi. Sherman's force spent five days tearing the town apart. A large detachment of infantry was detailed to destroy the railroads about the town so that they could not serve Confederate purposes for the rest of the war. The Federals also destroyed an arsenal, storehouses and other property, causing an estimated $50,000,000 in damage. On 20 February, Sherman headed west, and arrived safely in Canton six days later.

The raid had been almost a complete success. The Federals had managed to destroy the main rail lines of central Missis-

allowing the *Army of Tennessee* to sport only around 25,000 men at the beginning of the campaign. The force was led by Major General James B. McPherson, a rising star who was a protege of both Grant and Sherman.

The smallest contingent in Sherman's command was the *Army of the Ohio*. This army was little more than the over-glorified *XXIII Corps* consisting of 13,000 men under the command of the untested Major General John M. Schofield.

During March, the *Army of the Cumberland* remained in Chattanooga, the *Army of the Ohio* was near Knoxville and the *Army of the Tennessee* was stationed at Vicksburg. By Spring, these forces had been consolidated near Chattanooga. By early May, Sherman's forces were ready for the long-awaited campaign against Johnston.

sippi and paralyze the Confederate forces in the area. One hundred miles of track had been destroyed and a swath of destruction, 50 miles wide, had been cut across the state of Mississippi. The only major failure of the campaign was the defeat of Sooy Smith's cavalry at the hands of Forrest and his men.

More importantly however, Sherman's Meridian escapade had proven the success of the raid, if properly executed. After the Atlanta campaign, Sherman would use the destructive raid to accomplish what became known as the strategy of exhaustion. In effect, this entailed the destruction of the Confederacy's ability to support its armies and the will of its people to fight.

Yankee foragers loot the farm of a Confederate citizen during the Meridian raid. When the raid was over, Sherman's army left a swath of destruction almost 50 miles wide between Vicksburg and Meridian.

Booty of war. A sizable display of Rebel artillery pieces captured during the battles of Chattanooga outside the headquarters of the Army of the Cumberland.

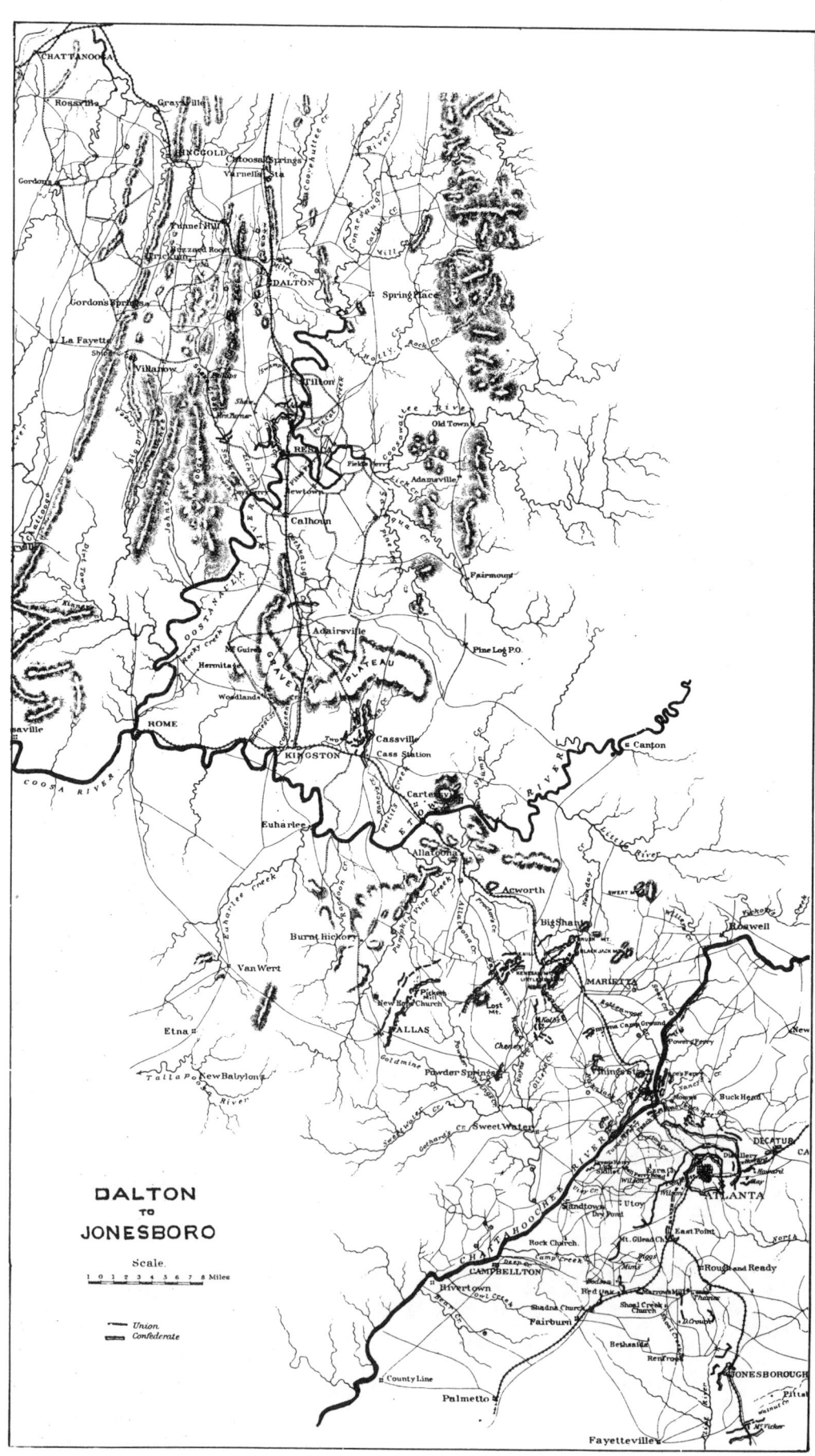

DALTON TO JONESBORO

Red River Campaign

The Red River campaign was one of the most ill-conceived and disastrous Federal operations of the entire Civil War. Given the scope of some Union disasters, such as First Bull Run, Second Bull Run, Fredericksburg and New Market, this may seem an unfounded claim. However, the fact that a small Confederate detachment easily routed a greatly superior force of Yankees should prove the Red River campaign's primacy in the ranks of National military dishonor.

Major General Nathaniel Banks was probably one of the Union's worst generals. He had a long record of ignominious defeats: Stonewall Jackson had literally run circles around him in the valley in 1862, he had presided over the Federal route at Cedar Mountain in August of that year, he led the disastrous attempt to take Galveston and blundered the campaign against Port Hudson in 1863. Banks' former position as governor of Massachusetts and his influence as a prominent Republican kept him in military command although such inept handling of strategy and tactics would have led to the relief of any other commander early in the war.

As 1864, the third year of the war, dawned, Banks led a command of several thousand troops in New Orleans. Originally, Banks was to lead his troops in an expedition against the port city of Mobile, Alabama in May. This movement would preface a thrust into the interior of Alabama and Georgia, to coincide with Sherman's assault from Chattanooga. However, military and political planners seized upon the idea of using Banks' idle force during the late winter and early spring to embark on a campaign into the Trans-Mississippi, up the Red River and into the interior of Louisiana.

Various leaders had great ideas for such a campaign. Grant was interested in the move because it would drive the Confederates from the Mississippi and free up the garrisons that protected its river traffic. Lincoln was interested as well, for meant the occupation of most of Louisiana, which could then be reconstructed into a free state. Banks also had a political stake in the campaign for his activities would enable Northern agents to buy or appropriate Louisiana cotton for mills in his native Massachusetts. Actually, the maneuver had little military value. The seizure of Vicksburg, which sealed the Mississippi for the Union, had already cut the rest of the Confederacy off from the industry, trade, supplies and troops of the Trans-Mississippi. The entire campaign was fueled by the prospect of enticing political and economic gains, rather than goals that would bring the war closer to an end.

Banks would command a sufficient force to allow him an achieve victory. With some 30,000 men and a flotilla of gunboats under the talented and capable Admiral David Dixon Porter, the general was to advance up the Red River into the heart of Louisiana, seize the headquarters of the Confederate Trans-Mississippi De-

A Confederate army under Lieutenant General Richard Taylor falls upon the Federal XIII Corps, Louisiana near Mansfield on 8 April. The Federals managed to hold for about an hour, but were then routed and driven from the field. Despite the arrival of reinforcements, the Federals were unable to turn Taylor's tide of victory.

partment, and destroy Confederate authority and power in the Pelican State. Ten thousand of Banks' troops, under Brigadier General A. J. Smith were on loan from Sherman's command. A supporting movement would be launched into Louisiana from Arkansas with 10,000 men under Major General Frederick Steele. Banks' troops were also reinforced with a detachment of traders armed with special permits that would allow them to trade with the enemy for cotton, which they could then sell in the North for hefty profits.

Though Banks was supposed to launch his offensive by early March, he delayed to celebrate the inauguration of the reconstructed government of Louisiana in New Orleans. Sherman was visiting the Crescent City at the time and later wrote of Banks' extensive plans in his memoirs:

> In Lafayette Square I saw the arrangements of scaffolding for the fireworks and benches for the audience. General Banks urged me to remain over the 4th of March, to participate in the ceremonies, which he explained would include the performance of the "Anvil Chorus" by all the bands of his army, and during the performance the church bells were to be rung, and cannons were to be fired by electricity. I regarded all such ceremonies as out of place at a time when it seemed to me every hour and every minute were due to the war.

Banks began his ill-fated campaign on 12 March by advancing his troops from Simmesport at the confluence of the Red and Mississippi rivers. At first, the Massachusetts political general enjoyed nothing but success. On the fourteenth, the Federals had advanced up the river to capture Fort DeRussy, and they took Alexandria on the fifteenth. By 3 April, Banks was in Grand Encore, preparing his push for Shreveport. However, to move on this city, the Federals would have to abandon the Red River and the protection of their gunboats and take to the roads between the Red and Sabine rivers going through Pleasant Hill and Mansfield.

As Banks moved further and further into the heartland of the Pelican State, his nerve began to waver and he became overly cautious. The movements of his army became slower and slower as he grew increasingly concerned about the possibility of a Confederate attack.

There was not much reason for Banks to be concerned. His only real opposition was the 7,000-man force under the command of Major General Richard B. Taylor. However, Taylor, son of President Zachary Taylor and brother-in-law to Jefferson Davis, was preparing to make a stand against the larger number of Federals moving against him. He planned to hit Banks' advancing column in the rough terrain of pine forests and rolling hills near Mansfield, where his smaller numbers would stand a better chance. The Confederates would enjoy further advantages because Banks' men would be strung out along the road leading from the Red River to Mansfield and Shreveport.

On 8 April, Taylor struck. His reinforced army of 8,800 men hit the Federal van guard of 5,720 men of the *XIII Corps* under Brigadier General Thomas E. G. Ransom three miles southeast of Mansfield. Though more troops of the *XIII Corps* arrived on the field during the battle, the Federals were eventually routed and driven back three miles to Pleasant Grove, where they were joined by a division of the *XIX Corps* under Brigadier General William H. Emory. There, the force attempted to make a stand. However, Confederates attacked at 1800 and pressed the Federals back even further, until the battle ended in the coming night. The Yankees had taken a thorough beating at Taylor's hands, losing 20 guns, 150 wagons with supplies, 1,000 horses, and 2,235 men, most of them captured. Taylor had only lost 1,000 men, even though he was on the attack. During the night, the Federals chose to fall back further still, to the town of Pleasant Hill, where Banks would attempt to create a defensive line against the attacking Confederates.

There Banks assembled a powerful force. In addition to the elements of the *XIII Corps* and *XIX Corps* which had

Banks' army crosses a bayou on its invasion into Louisiana during the Red River campaign.

Building An Offensive / 31

Confederates capture and loot a Federal wagon train after the rout of Banks' troops at the battle of Mansfield (also known as Sabine Crossroads) on 8 April. Taylor's men captured 150 wagons and 1,000 horses and mules after driving the Yankee foe from the battlefield.

fought on 8 April, two divisions of Brigadier General Andrew J. Smith's *XVI Corps* were also on hand along with two cavalry brigades. All in all, Banks had 12,000 men to continue the battle on the ninth. However, his line, on a plateau before Pleasant Hill, had been poorly planned and was not properly prepared to meet a harsh offensive. Gaps between some of the aligned brigades could be exploited to great benefit by the Confederates, if they chose to attack.

Taylor was all too willing to continue besting the Federals. His troop strength had been reinforced again and he had some 12,100 men before Pleasant Hill. Taylor had no reservations about using this force against an enemy that could possibly call upon stronger numbers. The Confederate general planned to take the offensive yet again, hitting the enemy in front and on his left flank, while a cavalry force would work to cut off the Yankee retreat.

Behind the Federal line of battle at Pleasant Hill on 9 April 1864. Though Banks was hardly outnumbered by Taylor's Confederate army and even managed to hold his own during the day of battle, the fray at Pleasant Hill caused the timorous Federal general to abandon his great Red River campaign.

The Confederate attack was delayed during the early morning and afternoon of the ninth, but finally got underway by 1700. The Confederate flanking force was unable to get on the Yankee left flank and had to attack the enemy front. While this attack was repulsed, the rest of Taylor's command was pitched into the battle and drove the Federals slowly back. After the attack had ended in the darkness of night, both sides left the battlefield; Taylor withdrew to find water for his men, and a beaten Banks retreated for the Red River. The Confederates had lost 1,626 men to Banks' 1,369 casualties. Despite this heavy toll, Taylor was more than willing to fight another day. However, Banks had enough of the campaign and was prepared to give up altogether and withdraw to his starting point.

The next few days saw the comical spectacle of Banks retreating for Alexandria with his force of 25,000, pursued by a force one-fifth the size under Richard Taylor. Taylor actually hoped to bag Banks' entire army, but his efforts were hampered by departmental commander Lieutenant General Kirby Smith. Smith was preoccupied with Steele's advance into Arkansas and requisitioned a substantial number of Taylor's troops to repel an advance which was already faltering. Thanks to Smith, Banks was probably saved further embarrassment and made Alexandria safely on 26 April. There his troops were reinforced to a strength of 31,000 men.

Banks was stalled at Alexandria for several weeks because the gunboat flotilla that he had brought with him was trapped on the Red River. The boats, which drew seven feet were blocked by waters which had fallen to a depth of three feet. Fortunately for the Federals, the gunboats did not have to be abandoned. An officer hit upon the idea of building jetties to narrow the river and raise the water level. Three thousand men were engaged in this endeavor, using expensive bales of cotton which were appropriated from the merchants who had accompanied Banks' on his ill-fated mission. The plan worked and the gunboats were able to sail to safety. By 13 May, Banks had extricated himself from Alexandria and seven days later, the farcical campaign was over.

The Red River fiasco had a definite impact on Sherman's Atlanta campaign. After Banks had become tied up in Louisiana, Grant was forced to admit that the forces employed in the Red River campaign would be unable to engage in operations east of the Mississippi that spring. This meant that Sherman would not only be deprived of the 10,000 men that he had lent Banks for his ill-fated operation but that all hopes of taking Mobile would have to be abandoned for the time being. Grant's plans of using both Banks' and Sherman's forces to bag Johnston were thus destroyed. Now, Johnston would be able to devote his full attention and energies to fielding Sherman's advance south from Chattanooga, making Federal success in Georgia all the more difficult. Sherman's campaign against Atlanta would be prolonged by weeks and even months, while large numbers of Federals died in painful battles with Johnston's men. The only positive result of the campaign was that Banks was relieved of field command and therefore would be unable to wreak his special brand of incompetence in any of the Union's future engagements.

Dams constructed across Red River at Alexandria, Louisiana to effect the crossing of Federal gunboats trapped by low waters.

CHAPTER III

ROCKY FACE RIDGE

7 May - 12 May, 1864

When Sherman set his troops into motion, Johnston's army was prepared to defy his advance from a strong position on Rocky Face Ridge just west of Dalton. The heights stretched for several miles from north to south running, roughly parallel to the Connasauga River. The ridge itself was a massive 700-foot barrier of quartz rock which blocked access into the interior of Georgia and the Western & Atlantic Railway. Its western face was an almost unassailable precipice. If it were occupied by even a small number of well-entrenched troops, a large army could only force its way beyond the ridge at a few points, with great difficulty and very probably with heavy casualties. Sherman correctly termed it "the terrible door of death."

Rocky Face Ridge only yielded a small number of gaps through which an army could pass. To the northwest of Dalton was Mill Creek Gap, called "Buzzard's Roost" by local citizens, where the Western & Atlantic passed through the mountain. Four or five miles to the south was Dug Gap and twelve miles to the south of this, just west of Resaca, was Snake Creek Gap.

Johnston drew up his line expecting an attack from the north, through the Crow Creek Valley east of Rocky Face Ridge and against Mill Creek and Dug Gaps. Hood's Corps guarded the northern extension of Johnston's line from the Crow Valley north of Dalton, up along the ridge, to the northern face of Mill Creek Gap. Hardee's Corps was divided, with Major General William Bate's Division occupying the southern face of Buzzard's Roost, extending south along Rocky Face Ridge, while Major General Patrick R. Cleburne's and Major General W. H. T. Walker's Divisions were in reserve at Resaca. Confederate cavalry was active on the north, west and rear of Johnston's line.

No doubt Johnston hoped the Federals would waste themselves on a direct assault against his formidable position. However, Sherman effectively found a way to circumvent Johnston's army. George Thomas learned from scouts that Snake Creek Gap had been incautiously left unguarded by the Confederates, and proposed to Sherman an ambitious plan to take advantage of the fateful opening; the *Army of the Cumberland* would advance through Snake Creek Gap and threaten the Confederate rear at Resaca

The terrain of Rock Face Ridge. The steep ascent of the ridge, thick foliage and numerous boulders played havoc with attacking Federal formations.

or Calhoun, while the rest of the Federal army would occupy Johnston's front. Sherman had originally envisioned a stab 40 miles towards the southwest against Rome, Georgia, but came to accept Thomas' idea. However, he decided to modify the move by having McPherson's command make the flanking maneuver and Thomas' force occupy Johnston's front with Schofield's troops. If all went according to plan, McPherson would be able to cut Johnston's supply line 15 miles south of Dalton at Resaca, force the retreat of his army from its strong position and cause it to fight a battle against stronger Federal numbers and on Federal terms.

There is much uncertainty as to why Johnston was so neglectful the defense of Snake Creek Gap. It is possible that he was unaware of its existence or believed that it would be impossible for an army to move through the pass. Divisional commander Cleburne bitterly wrote in a report after the fight for Rocky Face Ridge, "How this gap, which opened into our rear and line of communication, from which it was distant at Resaca only five miles, was neglected, I cannot imagine. General Mackall, Johnston's Chief-of-Staff, told me it was the result of a flagrant disobedience of orders—by whom he did not say. Certainly, the Commanding General never could have failed to appreciate its importance." However, Johnston did have reason to believe that he could meet any threat to his rear for Confederate reinforcements were arriving at Resaca. Lieutenant General Leonidas Polk's Army of Mississippi had been ordered by Richmond to reinforce the Army of Tennessee on 4 May and was on its way from Alabama to join Johnston. Polk, an Episcopalian Bishop turned fighting general, had left the Army of Tennessee due to a falling out with Bragg after Chickamauga, but was now returning to the force bringing some 14,000 with him. The first of Polk's command, a division under Brigadier General James Cantey, propitiously arrived in Resaca on 7 May as McPherson was moving on Snake Creek Gap. Though Cantey was supposed to bring his 4,000 troops north, to Dalton,

Battle is joined at the "terrible door of death," Buzzard's Roost Pass or Mill Creek Gap at Rocky Face Ridge. The Army of the Cumberland engaged Johnston's Confederate troops at Rocky Face Ridge while James B. McPherson's Army of the Tennessee maneuvered to get into the Confederate rear at Resaca.

Johnston had them remain at Resaca to cover the crossings over the Oostanaula River.

On 7 May, Sherman's troops had moved south and were demonstrating before Johnston's works at Rocky Face Ridge. Schofield's *Army of the Ohio* bore down on the Confederate right from the north while the *Army of Cumberland* moved into position to threaten Mill Creek Gap and Dug Gap. Confederate soldier Lot D. Young described the appearance and sound of the Federal advance before Rocky Face Ridge:

> We...took position...on the mountain [Rocky Face Ridge], from which we could see extending for miles his grand encampment of infantry and artillery, the stars and stripes floating from every regimental brigade, division and corps headquarters and presenting the greatest panorama I ever beheld. Softly and sweetly the music from their bands as they played the national airs were wafted up and over the summit of the mountain. Somehow, some way, in some inexplicable and unseen manner, 'Hail Columbia,' 'America' and 'The Star Spangled Banner' sounded sweeter than I had ever before heard them, and filled my soul with feelings that I could not describe or forget.

On the eighth, the *Army of the Cumberland* actively engaged Hood's troops on Rocky Face Ridge. Thomas' only success came when Brigadier General C. G. Harker's

Railroads During the Civil War

By 1861, the United States maintained a network of 31,000 miles of railroad track, providing the youthful nation with a cheap and efficient method of transporting its populace and commercial goods over its vast holdings of land from the Mississippi to the east coast and from Maine to the Gulf States. During the Civil War, lines throughout the United States attained immense strategic significance for both sides as logistical and operational use of railroads made the difference between victory and defeat.

Though the U.S. possessed thousands of miles of railroad track at the outbreak of the war, the rail system was still quite disorganized. There was no standard gauge in use throughout the U.S. at the time so rolling stock varied accordingly. Many lines, including those leading to major cities, were not connected to other significant routes, thus entailing a complex process of embarking and disembarking to get from one place to another. In numerous places, wooden rails with metal bands nailed down on top of them were used instead of iron rails, making the lines extremely dangerous and train wrecks common. Still, as war swept across the country, railways were constantly and successfully employed to transport troops and supply armies in the field.

Throughout the Civil War, railroads served as an efficient method of supplying huge armies with ammunition, food and other items. The importance of a railroad to a Civil War army is best understood by comparing it with another common form of transportation of the time, the wagon. A large force of 50,000 men, comprised of 40,000 infantry, 7,500 cavalry, 2,500 cannoneers, 200 artillery pieces, 10,000 horses and mules would need at least 215 tons of rations to feed all its troops and livestock. For wagons to support this force even for a short time and over a short distance would require an immense amount of effort. The standard army wagon of the day could only carry 1.5 tons of supplies. A crew of three teamsters and 12 mules worked a pair of wagons employed. These had to be fed as well, adding 10 more tons to the needed by the army. These extra supplies had to be carried by more wagons, whose crews and teams also required sustenance, sending the amount of equipment, personnel and livestock necessary to support the army into an upwards spiral. The total amount needed to transport supplies reaches a hefty total of 153 wagons, around 230 men and 918 mules to supply 50,000 men just 10 miles away from its supply base for only one day. If the army was even farther away from its supply line, the figure would increase substantially. If the force in question happened to operate just 20 miles from its base, it would then require 312 wagons, 468 men and 1,872 mules, taking two days to make the round trip. If the army operated from a maximum distance of 50 miles away, it would require 1,520 wagons, 2,300 men and over 9,000 animals for the five day journey to its destination and back. Though these calculations document the immense difficulty in transporting supplies by wagon, they actually underestimate the needs of the Civil War army. They fail to take into account the large amounts of ammunition and other supplies needed to keep an army in the field, as well as the vulnerability of a long wagon train to enemy raids.

In simple terms, trains were ten times cheaper than wagon transportation in supplying an army. For the 215 tons required by an army of 50,000 some 50 miles away, all that was needed was a locomotive, a couple of tenders, seventeen cars and a crew of six. Obviously, this was much less than the resources needed to move such supplies by wagon. Thus the train improved the efficiency, ability and range of the modern Civil War army.

The critical importance of rail transportation for the logistical support of an army was clearly in evidence during the Atlanta campaign. With Sherman operating hundreds of miles from his main supply bases and no navigable rivers to allow transportation of supplies by boat, the Federal general was forced to stick close to the Western & Atlantic Railroad from Chattanooga to Atlanta. For most of the campaign, this line dictated the path of Sherman's advance.

As Sherman moved on Atlanta, the rails in Tennessee and Georgia hummed with activity. Sixteen trains of ten cars each ran to Sherman's army daily carrying 1,600 tons of supplies, swelling his depots with more than enough goods to supply the Federal offensive and allow for rail accidents. In his memoirs, Sherman wrote of the importance of rail transportation to his campaign, "The Atlanta campaign would simply have been impossible without the use of railroads...."

Railroads also played an important operational role in many of the great campaigns of the war. The ability to move thousands of troops quickly to various areas decided between victory and defeat on numerous occasions. The first use of railroads for military operational purposes took place early in the Civil War, at First Bull Run on 21 July 1861. A few days before the battle, Brigadier General Joseph E. Johnston had his 12,000-man force entrain in the Shenandoah Valley, to travel along the Manassas Gap Railroad to Manassas. Johnston's forces then joined Brigadier General P. G. T. Beauregard's army to defeat a Federal legion under Irwin McDowell. Thenceforth, railroads were a prominent factor in many of the campaigns of the Civil War.

The most spectacular movements by both sides during the war took place just before and after the battle of Chickamauga (19-20 September). Before the battle, James Longstreet's Corps of the Army of Northern Virginia was temporarily transferred west to Braxton Bragg's Army of Tennessee. The Federal seizure of Knoxville and Chattanooga in 1863 deprived the Confederates of a 550-mile direct rail route to Bragg's army. Thus,

Iron horses of the Federal armies in the West. These five locomotives were built by soldiers at Vicksburg, Mississippi under the direction of a member of Major General James B. McPherson's staff.

Longstreet's men were funneled through the logistical nightmare of the inferior Confederate rail system. Due to the lack of contiguous rails and the different gauges in track, the entire movement involved some seventeen days of constant entraining and detraining of the 12,000 men, as well as large amounts of ordnance, livestock and supplies. To get to Bragg's army, the Confederates traveled through the Carolinas, Augusta, Atlanta, and thence to Northern Georgia, covering 965 miles on 16 different railroads. Despite the immense difficulties, enough of Longstreet's men arrived on the field of battle at Chickamauga to wring a victory out of the bloody contest.

However, the Federals were not to be outdone by Confederate efforts. After the *Army of the Cumberland* was routed from the field at Chickamauga, it was besieged by the Bragg's Army of Tennessee at Chattanooga. In order to save the beleaguered army, reinforcements in the form of two corps from the *Army of the Potomac* were sent west under the command of Joseph Hooker in late September. The transportation of these troops by rail almost dwarfed Longstreet's exertions earlier in the month. Hooker's force of 25,000 men, 10 batteries of artillery and 3,000 horses and mules traveled 1,157 miles to their destination of East Tennessee in just twelve days, making the operation the greatest rail movement up to that time.

Sherman also paid homage to the operational uses of the railroad during the Atlanta campaign when he struck at the Georgia Railroad shortly after crossing the Chattahoochee in mid-July of 1864. The move effectively stifled any chance of Lee's Army of Northern Virginia and Johnston's Army of Tennessee from supporting each other, as the Confederates had been able to do almost a year earlier.

Cut off from a railroad, a Civil War army would be forced to retreat. Evidence of this was displayed on numerous occasions during the war. A day after Federal troops cut the lifeline of the Army of Northern Virginia, the South Side Railroad, Lee's command was forced to give up the Petersburg and Richmond and begin a long march that would finally end in surrender. With Sherman's destruction of the railroads around Atlanta, Hood was forced to fall back from the town and retreat to safety. Both these incidents serve as salient examples of the importance of the railroad to the Civil War army.

brigade of the *IV Corps* managed to scale the northern face of Rocky Face Ridge and advance south along its crest. The National troops rooted out Confederate outposts and skirmishers and managed to close in on Buzzard's Roost. About a mile and a half north of the gap, Harker's men stalled due to difficult terrain and a strong Confederate position.

Four miles to the south, Brigadier General John W. Geary's Division of Hooker's *XX Corps* engaged 250 Arkansasians and Kentuckians holding Dug Gap. The attack was made over a treacherous rocky incline covered with tangled growth. Advances were only be possible in a few places, through clefts where five or six men could barely march abreast. As the Federals scaled the ridge, the Southerners peppered them with bullets and rolled large rocks down into the Yankee ranks with deadly effect. Some Federal regiments began to suffer a heavy toll. Company G of the *33d New Jersey* lost its captain, and then its first lieutenant. After the unit's second lieutenant took command, he let out an "unearthly" scream and fled from the combat with his wounded arm dangling by his side. The spectacle earned the morbid laughter of his comrades. Though the Federals managed to get in close to the Confederate line and engage in hand-to-hand combat in some places, no significant gains could be made. Rather than pursue the ineffectual offensive any further, Geary's troops opted to take cover. The division lost 49 dead, 357 wounded and 51 missing during the engagement, while the Confederates only suffered about 50 casualties.

The next day, members of the Harker's brigade attempted to force their way further

Dug Gap, the scene of an attack by Federals of Geary's Division of the XX Corps against a small detachment of Arkansas infantry and dismounted Kentucky cavalry.

south. Two guns had been brought up to assist the attack, but the chance of winning any more ground on the narrow summit of the ridge in the face of the well-entrenched Rebels was almost non-existent. Brigadier General Jacob Cox watched the assault from Schofield's position north of Crow Valley. He later wrote:

> The line of blue coats could be seen among the rocks, nearly at right angles with the line of the ridge, the men at the top in *silhouette* against the sky, close up to the Confederate trenches, where their charges were met with a line of fire before which they recoiled only to renew the effort, till it became apparent even to the most daring that it was useless to lead men up against such barriers. The orders were not to waste life in serious assault upon entrenchments, but the zeal of the troops and subordinate commanders turned the intended skirmish into something very like a ranged battle....

The *Army of the Ohio* also attempted to engage the Confederates on the ninth by testing their entrenchments in the Crow Valley. Schofield's Federals found the Rebel works too strong to achieve a breakthrough, and were repulsed.

While most of Sherman's army engaged Johnston's command in a series of costly skirmishes, the *Army of the Tennessee* undertook a flanking maneuver against Resaca via the Snake Creek Gap. In early May, McPherson's troops struck out for the south

Federals of Geary's division assail Confederate positions at Dug Gap.

and turned west through Taylor's Ridge at Ship's Gap for Villanow. After passing through the crossroads town, it headed southwest to reach Snake Creek Gap. Most of the long march was screened from the Confederates by Taylor's Ridge, a prominence running roughly parallel to Rocky Face Ridge. On late 8 May, the *Army of the Tennessee* had arrived at Snake Creek Gap and was posted in an advantageous position to assail Johnston's rear and threaten the Confederate line of communications and supply at Resaca.

Though the flanking movement had been hidden in the mountains to the west of the Confederate line at Rocky Face Ridge, Johnston had and lost an opportunity to divine the threat before it could seriously endanger him. In fact, Major General Joseph Wheeler's cavalry had been ordered to scout west of Taylor's Ridge on 5 May, a move which surely would have exposed Sherman's planned surprise. However, due to some mishap, the order was miswritten so as to detail a useless cavalry reconnaissance east of Taylor's Ridge. Despite this comedy of error, the Confederates still had the opportunity to discover and meet McPherson's advance. Though Johnston's headquarters began to receive word of the *Army of the Tennessee*'s march on Snake Creek Gap later in the week, Johnston misinterpreted these reports as referring to Geary's attack against Dug Gap or a Federal movement on Rome.

Early on 9 May, McPherson advanced from the Snake Creek Gap and by the late afternoon was within a few miles of the town of Resaca and ever so close to victory. However, the Federal general was finding his advantageous position in the Rebel rear

Federal troops seize an almost undefended Snake Creek Gap on 8 May 1864. Once in possession of the vital pass, McPherson was able to advance almost unmolested into the Confederate rear thus making Johnston's position on the formidable Rocky Face Ridge untenable.

James B. McPherson
1828-1864

Major General James B. McPherson was one of the brightest rising stars in the ranks of Federal command and probably would have won a significant place in American history if his life had not been cut short by a Rebel minie ball at the battle of Atlanta, on 22 July.

Born in Ohio in 1828, McPherson found responsibility thrust upon his shoulders at an early age when he was forced to support his family because his father was declared mentally incompetent. McPherson first found work as a store clerk and so impressed his employer that he helped the lad find an education at the Norwalk Academy. He later gained acceptance to West Point, in 1849 at the comparatively mature age of 21, and graduated four years later at the top of his class. His years preceding the war were occupied by a teaching post at the Military Academy and work on improvements to harbors and coastal fortifications.

After the war broke out, McPherson was employed by some of the leading figures who emerged from the Federal Western theater of operations. In November of 1861, he was a lieutenant colonel and aide de camp to Major General Henry Halleck, who was engaged in bringing order to the Department of Missouri after John C. Fremont's escapades as commander there. A few months later, in February, he served Ulysses S. Grant as the chief engineer in the *Army of the Tennessee* during the battles of Fort

Major General James B. McPherson

Henry, Fort Donelson, Shiloh and Corinth.

McPherson's fortunes rapidly progressed over the next few months. He was promoted to colonel and then brigadier general, and was given a brigade of engineers which he commanded in the *Army of the Tennessee*. By October, McPherson was a major general with divisional command in the *XIII Corps*, and in December was appointed the helmsman of the *XVII Corps*.

McPherson commanded the *XVII Corps* throughout Grant's Vicksburg campaign, winning overwhelming respect from Grant and fellow commander Major General William T. Sherman. In March of 1864, when Sherman was appointed to the command of the armies charged with the Military Division of the Mississippi and detailed with the task of driving against Johnston and Atlanta, McPherson was given charge of the *Army of the Tennessee*, which he would lead throughout the Atlanta campaign, until his untimely death. At first, McPherson did not live up to his promising reputation. He failed to take Resaca and post himself in Johnston's rear early in the campaign. Despite this disappointment, McPherson performed ably for the rest of the advance for Atlanta. On 22 July, McPherson's career was brought to an end when he blundered into an advancing mass of Confederates and was shot down as he tried to escape. The death was all the more tragic since the young general was engaged to marry a belle of Baltimore.

McPherson's abilities were lauded by the best Federal commanders of the war, Grant and Sherman. Sherman even went as far as to remark, "If he lives, he'll outdistance Grant and myself." McPherson's death came as a great shock to his commander during the Atlanta campaign. It has been said that Sherman wept when he saw McPherson's body after it was recovered from the battlefield.

---

not at all pleasing. First, reconnaissance and captured Confederates told of a strong Rebel force holding Resaca. This information was confirmed by increased Southern resistance as the Federals closed on the town. Second, McPherson was overly concerned that Johnston might ignore the forces occupying his front and fall with all his might on the *Army of the Tennessee*. Unaware of the situation confronting the rest of Sherman's army, McPherson decided to adopt what seemed to be the most prudent course of action and retreated to safety at Snake Creek Gap.

When Sherman learned that McPherson had gotten through Snake Creek Gap, he exclaimed, "I've got Joe Johnston dead." However, his enthusiasm was substantially deflated when he learned of McPherson's failure to take Resaca. Disappointed, but undaunted by his subordinate's lack of success, Sherman had the *Army of the Ohio* and the *Army of the Cumberland* move south to join the *Army of the Tennessee* at Snake Creek Gap. Hooker's corps was to take the lead on the 10 May, followed by the rest of the army over the next two days, while Howard's division of Hooker's corps would remain north of Dalton. When Sherman met with McPherson at Snake Creek Gap, he reminded his protege of the lost chance of glory by saying, "Well, Mac, you missed the opportunity of your life!"

In the Confederate camp, Johnston was slow to react to the Federal activity that was posing an increasingly dangerous threat to his rear. When the Confederate general learned of Federal action near Resaca, he responded by sending Hood south to the town with Major General Thomas C. Hindman's Division and Cleburne's and Walker's divisions of Hardee's Corps. Arriving in the vicinity of Resaca on 10 May, Hood found that the Federals had retreated. Johnston then ordered Hood to return North with Hindman's Division and to post Cleburne's and Walker's midway between Dalton and Resaca, at Tilton. Evidently, Johnston still thought the major Federal thrust would fall upon him north of Dalton.

Two days after he had dispatched Hood on his short reconnaissance, Johnston came to the realization that the Federals were in fact threatening to move on Resaca. As the majority of Sherman's army was on its way south, the Confederate general was already receiving disturbing reports that the Federals were massing in the vicinity of Snake Creek Gap. On 12 May, Johnston sent Wheeler with his cavalry to investigate the National forces in front of Rocky Face Ridge. The reconnaissance mission revealed that only a token Federal force remained in the front of the Army of Tennessee.

With this knowledge, Johnston could no longer hold on to his formidable position on Rocky Face Ridge. If he was to protect his connections with the rest of the South, the Army of Tennessee had to fall back to Resaca to cover the vital crossings over the Oostanaula River. Thus, Johnston set his army in motion toward Resaca on the night of 12 May. Upon his arrival at the town at 1000 the next day, Johnston's ranks would be swelled by reinforcements from Polk's command. Major General William W. Loring's Division, with the "Fighting Bishop" himself, arrived north of the Oostanaula to join Cantey on 10-11 May.

Though Sherman had forced his adversary to abandon his strong position at Rocky Face Ridge, his favorite subordinate, McPherson had bungled a "once in a lifetime" opportunity to seriously cripple the Army of Tennessee. Still, Sherman, at Resaca was more than willing to engage in a similar strategy to that which he had employed at Rocky Face Ridge and threaten Johnston's rear in order to either drive him back or destroy him.

CHAPTER IV

RESACA

12 May - 16 May, 1864

*A*s the Federal and Confederate commanders moved their armies south from Rocky Face Ridge, both had reason to feel embittered: Sherman had lost an unparalleled opportunity to bag his enemy through McPherson's caution; while Johnston had been forced to relinquish one of the most formidable positions he would hold during the campaign without inflicting any grave punishment upon the enemy. Both generals hoped to redeem their fortunes when they sought and entered battle outside of Resaca.

Johnston prepared to meet the Federals outside of Resaca by placing his army north and west of the town with his flanks on the Oostanaula and Connasauga rivers and partly along Camp Creek, a tributary of the Oostanaula running west of the town. Polk occupied the left with some of his troops on high hills dominating the ground east of Camp Creek in advance of his main line; Hardee occupied the center with his line extending north; Hood was on his right in a position which stretched east to the Connasauga. Though the Confederate position appeared to be quite strong, it also contained a serious defect which could possibly lead to a major disaster. Johnston's back was against the Oostanaula River. If the Federals managed to break through any point in Johnston's line, a successful retreat would be difficult to accomplish, and the entire Confederate Army of Tennessee might be trapped on the river bank.

On the thirteenth, Sherman's forces advanced out of Snake Creek Gap to fall upon Resaca, with McPherson in the lead. The Federals spent most of the day skirmishing with the Confederates and driving in tenacious Rebel pickets. As McPherson's movement became stalled by the increasing Southern resistance, the rest of the Northern command shifted to the north, to go on to the *Army of the Tennessee*'s left. By the evening, Sherman's line was set up almost parallel to Johnston's lines. McPherson took up a position opposite Polk with his right flank resting on the Oostanaula. On his left was the *Army of the Cumberland* followed by the *Army of the Ohio*. Howard's division advanced on Resaca from the north in the wake of Johnston's retreat, to come up on the left of Schofield.

Sherman intended to attack the Confederates the next day by having McPherson

Site of one of the first major confrontations of the Atlanta Campaign, the town of Resaca.

engage the Johnston's left, while Thomas and Schofield sought to achieve some success on their right. When Sherman inspected his lines before Resaca, his troops crowded around him in the hopes of learning something of his plans for the coming battle. "Take it easy to-day, for you will have work enough to-morrow," was all the information the general chose to give.

The Federal attack against Johnston's Resaca position began not long after mid-day on 14 May, with Schofield's *XXIII Corps* and Major General John M. Palmer's *XIV Corps* of the *Army of the Cumberland* under way against the Confederate right. The Federal advance was made over broken terrain of ravines and creek beds which severely hampered the progress of the advancing columns. Cox, on Schofield's left, managed to get his troops across Camp Creek and charged a portion of Hardee's line with bayonets fixed. The attack rooted the Rebels from their advance works and drove them back several yards. Cox's troops then came under a severe fire from the front and flank and were forced him to halt before they could exploit their gains.

Brigadier General Henry M. Judah's division on Schofield's right encountered much more difficulty. Poor coordination allowed the *First Brigade* of the division under Brigadier General Nathaniel C. McLean to become intertwined with elements from Palmer's *XIV Corps*. The confused mass advanced while another of Judah's brigades, Brigadier General Milo S. Hascall's, was accidentally left behind. The combined elements of Judah's division and Palmer's corps struggled through a forest and then marched over an open field to assail a steep hill across Camp Creek held by the Confederates. Once out in the open, the Federals were swept by a terrible fire of cannons and musketry. With his first attack crumbling under the heavy fire, Judah then sent Hascall's brigade into the fray, Despite the many reinforcements, the Federals were still unable to make any headway and the attack gradually expired as Schofield's and Palmer's men suffered heavy casualties. Judah's mishandling of the assault on 14 May would lead to his replacement by Hascall.

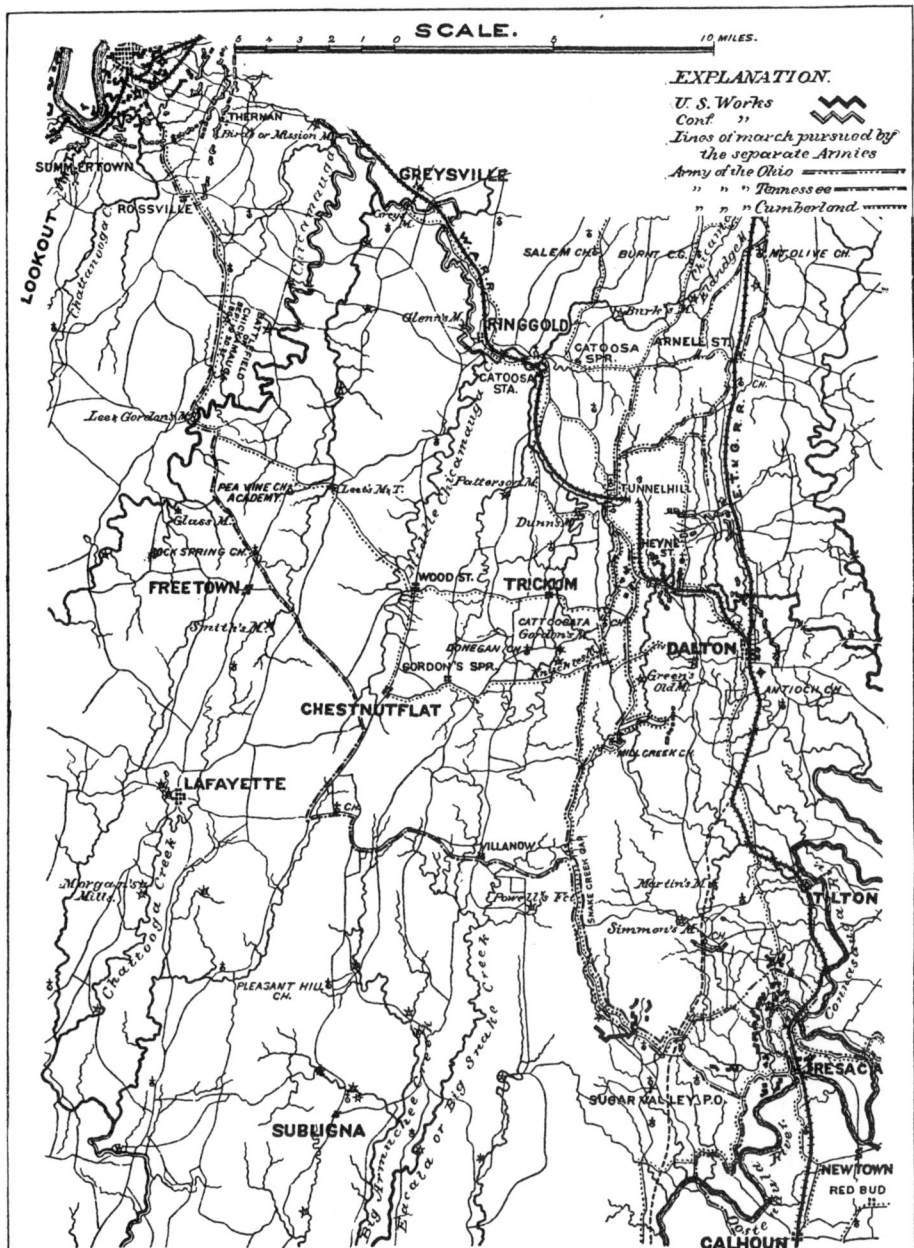

Map of action at Rocky Face Ridge and Resaca.

During the afternoon, the Confederates noticed a weakness in the Federal line and launched an attack of their own. Confederate cavalry reported to Johnston that the extreme Federal left was dangerously unprotected and vulnerable to a flank attack. Johnston decided to seize the opportunity and directed Hood to take Major General A. P. Stewart's and Major General C. L. Stevenson's divisions and hit the exposed National position. It was an assault that seemed to be made for Hood as he was a military fighter known for dealing out harsh blows.

Hood landed his attack on the Federal left at 1600 and drove off several brigades in a panic. While its infantry supports fled for the rear, the *5th Indiana Battery* remained on the field to defy the Confederate advance, pouring deadly blasts of double shotted canister into the Southern lines. Hood's troops advanced clearly disconcerted about approaching the Federal guns as they belched forth killing volleys of hot iron. For a while, the Southerners were held at bay though some Rebels managed to get within 50 feet of the guns before being forced back.

Any success Hood achieved was to prove short lived. The Federals were also aware of the frailty of their left and that afternoon had sent reinforcements to the area in the form of elements of Hooker's *XX Corps*. As soldiers from the *Army of the Potomac*,

John M. Schofield
1831-1906

Born in Gerry, New York, John M. Schofield proved a promising soldier at West Point, graduating seventh in his class. Although he saw military service with the *1st Artillery* in Florida, his years before the Civil War were spent more in pedantic pursuits, as a teacher of philosophy at the Military Academy, and a physics professor at Washington College at St. Louis, Missouri while on leave from the army.

Joining up with Brigadier General Nathaniel Lyon's Union forces in Missouri, Schofield served that commander as a staff officer. When Lyon sought battle against a larger Confederate force at Wilson's Creek, Schofield's counsel against the move was ignored and an assault was launched; Lyon was killed as he led his men forward, and the Federals were defeated.

Schofield was appointed a brigadier general in November of 1861, but his service was relegated to mundane duties in the Midwest, such as fighting against enemy guerrillas in Kansas and Missouri. After intense lobbying, Schofield won a major generalcy in May of 1863 and in February of 1864, command of the *Army of the Ohio*, which he would lead during the Atlanta campaign. During Sherman's advance on Atlanta, Schofield commanded his small army, which was actually little more than a corps, with extraordinary competence.

After Sherman left with the *Army of the Tennessee* for the March to the Sea, Schofield's *Army of the Ohio* remained in the West, where it contested John B. Hood's advance into Tennessee. In the process it was almost cut off from the rest of the Federal forces then located at Nashville, but Schofield was able to escape to Franklin, where his troops dealt a bloody repulse to a Confederate attack on 30 November 1864. Schofield then retreated to join Major General George H. Thomas' *Army of the Cumberland* at Nashville, where Hood was defeated in December. Schofield later saw service with Sherman during his campaign in the Carolinas, as the commander of the Department of North Carolina.

After the war, Schofield enjoyed a series of successful political, military and diplomatic positions. He commanded the First Military District of Virginia, was sent to France to negotiate the removal of that country's troops from Mexico, and served as Andrew Johnson's secretary of war for a short period of time. He later served as the superintendent of West Point and took over the post of commanding general of the army from compatriot Philip Sheridan in 1888.

---

the Easterners had endured much abuse from their comrades in the *Army of the Cumberland*. The western Federals maintained that the defeats in Virginia had resulted from the fact that the soldiers of the *Army of the Potomac* were more interested in tending to their appearance than in hard fighting. For many months, Hooker's troops suffered from insults such as "All quiet on the Potomac," "Hello, paper collar soldiers," and "Hadn't you better stop and blacken your shoes." As Hooker's lead division under Brigadier General Alpheus S. Williams began to encounter their western comrades fleeing from the imperiled left, Williams repaid the absconding Cumberlanders for their earlier insults by shouting that a division of the *Army of the Potomac* had arrived to protect them. The eastern troops plowed into Hood's men, forcing the Confederates to retreat and saving the cannons of the *5th Indiana* from capture just as the Rebels prepared to take them in flank.

As the situation on the Confederate right degenerated into a stalemate of bloody attacks and counterattacks, Sherman came to enjoy considerable success in threatening the Confederate left. Troops from Brigadier General Peter J. Osterhaus' division of Major General John A. Logan's *XV Corps* of the *Army of the Tennessee* managed to secure a crossing over Camp Creek and threaten the rear of the Confederate troops entrenched on the prominence in advance of Polk's line. Around 1700-1800, Logan pushed Polk's Rebels off the hill with an attack by the brigades of Brigadier Generals Giles A. Smith and C. R. Woods. Polk attempted to retake the position, but was

Columns of Schofield's Army of the Ohio *storm Confederate entrenchments on the first day of battle at Resaca on 14 May 1864.*

unable to deprive Logan's troops of their gains. The hill was to prove an ideal position for Sherman as it overlooked the railroad and wagon bridges across the Oostanaula at Resaca. Once cannons were placed there, Johnston's primary crossings over the river would be vulnerable to artillery bombardment. However, Johnston side-stepped the Federal threat by directing his engineers to lay pontoon bridges further off up stream, out of the range of the enemy's guns.

The greatest Federal success of 14 May would not be won on the actual field of battle but to the southwest, where Sherman attempted to put a force in Johnston's rear as he had done at Resaca. The *Second Division* of the *XVI Corps* of the *Army of the Tennessee* under Brigadier General Thomas W. Sweeny had been sent several miles downstream to cross the Oostanaula at Lay's Ferry. Upon arrival at the ferry, the Federals found the crossing point guarded by a force of entrenched infantry and a battery of artillery. To circumvent this force, division commander Sweeny decided to have a brigade occupy the Southern troops at the ferry while another detachment sought to cross the river 300 yards downstream, where the Snake Creek entered the Oostanaula. All went according to plan. Despite heavy casualties, the Confederates were held at Lay's Ferry while the *66th Illinois* and *81st Ohio* regiments crossed the river and drove off the Butternut troops on the opposite bank.

Although Sweeny had established a bridgehead which provided access into the Confederate rear, Sherman decided to abandon the mission to cross the Oostanaula for the time being. Both Sherman and Sweeny had received reports that Southern forces were converging on the exposed Federals on the southern bank of the river. In response, the exposed troops were quickly recalled and forced to abandon the bridgehead which they had worked all afternoon to achieve. As it turned out, Johnston had learned of a possible threat to the south on the fourteenth and had dispatched W. H.

Johnston's Confederate line thwarts a Union attack at Resaca on 14 and 15 May 1864. While the Federals were unable to win any major successes on the actual battlefield, Sherman was able flank the Army of Tennessee's position by getting some of his forces across the Chattahoochee to threaten the Southern rear.

T. Walker's division to investigate. Finding the Yankees had recrossed the stream, Walker reported that there was no immediate threat at Lay's Ferry.

The next day, Sherman renewed the offensive by having Hooker attack Hood on the Confederate right. Despite some initial confusion, Hooker's assault was under way by 1130. Though the assault was repulsed, a small victory was achieved when troops led by the commander of the *70th Indiana*, future president Benjamin Harrison, descended upon a small fort in advance of the Confederate line and seized the guns of Max Van Den Corput's Georgia battery posted there. Unfortunately, the Southern fire proved too hot for the Yankees to either hold the fort or safely steal the captured guns back to friendly lines. However, the Federals were loathe to give up such trophies as Confederate artillery. Under cover of darkness, during the night of 15 May, they returned for the guns, cutting a hole in the wall of the fort and pulling them out from the breach with ropes.

To the south, Sweeny's men were at work crossing the Oostanaula once more. The Federals repeated their performance of the day before and won similar results. With the opposite bank secure, Sweeny had a pontoon bridge laid and crossed the river with the rest of his division. Once again, as at Rocky Face Ridge, Johnston was to find a serious danger in his rear, threatening his supply lines.

Throughout the fourteenth and the fifteenth, Johnston vacillated over whether to launch another attack against the Federal left. He was satisfied by Hood's short lived victory on the fourteenth and prepared to launch a similar onslaught the next day. However, when he received word that the Federals were crossing the Oostanaula to the south, Johnston decided to call off the attack while Walker investigated the enemy activity. When Walker reported that the Federals were not across the river, Johnston changed his mind and gave Hood the go ahead to take the offensive. However, when Walker later reported Sweeny's recrossing, the commander of the Army of Tennessee changed his mind yet again and called off the assault. In all this confusion a mishap occurred. One of Hood's divisions under Stewart failed to receive word that the attack had been canceled. Thus, at 1600 he advanced his division, only to find himself without proper support and suffered a bloody repulse in a tragic and fruitless assault.

By the night of the fifteenth, Johnston found his position at Resaca in serious danger. With a strong Federal force poised to fall on the Army of Tennessee's lifeline, the Western & Atlantic, Johnston was forced to retreat his army across the Oostanaula towards Calhoun. At 0330 on 16 May, the bridges at Resaca were torched to delay the inevitable pursuit by Sherman's army.

Sherman entered the vacated Resaca the next day, on 16 May. He quickly sent his forces across the river to follow Johnston and engage in the next series of confrontations. As the Confederate retreat had abandoned Rome, Georgia, Sherman sent Brigadier General Jefferson C. Davis' division of the *XIV Corps* of the *Army of the Cumberland* and troopers of Brigadier General Kenner Garrard's cavalry division to seize the town and deprive the Confederate war machine of its factories and iron works. The Federals took Rome after losing 150 men in a fight with a detachment of Rebels on 18 May. Davis would rejoin the rest of the army when it was outside of Dallas, over a week later.

Though Resaca was hardly a costly conflict by Civil War standards, the soldiers witnessed horrifying and moving scenes. After the battle, a visitor to the fort where Harrison's men had fought wrote:

Members of Logan's XV Corps *drive back elements of Polk's command on the first day of the battle of Resaca. Logan's assault forced the Confederates to abandon a vital prominence overlooking Johnston's crossings over the Chattahoochee.*

Inside and around the work rebel and Union officers and men lay piled together; some transfixed with bayonet wounds, their faces wearing that fierce, contorted look that marks those who have suffered agony. Others, who were shot dead, lay with their calm and glassy eyes turned toward heaven. One might have thought they were sleeping.

Another Federal found on the body of one Southern soldier orders from his conscription officer detailing him to leave his home and family and join the army just two weeks before the fight at Resaca. He remembered of this body:

> I have seen fields of battle in front of our regiment, covered over with the dead, without experiencing the pang of regret that I felt for this poor lad who, scarcely out from home, and too frightened and confused to know what to do, thus sadly met his fate.

The soldiers of the *27th Indiana* stumbled upon a pitiful sight. Near a crude log hut which had been converted into a field hospital during the battle, the troops discovered amputated arms and limbs stacked like cord wood. A wounded major still lay upon an operating table, abandoned mid-way through his operation by a surgeon loathe to be caught behind the Confederate retreat. The pain from his wound was so great that he begged his captors to shoot him.

The first phase of Sherman's campaign had been a complete success. Johnston had

Federal guns shell the Western & Atlantic Railroad and the bridges spanning the Chattahoochee at Resaca.

Resaca / 51

Under cover of darkness, Yankees of Geary's division retrieve cannons from a Confederate fort captured earlier in the day by troops under Colonel Benjamin Harrison, a future president.

been forced to relinquish his strong position on Rocky Face Ridge without a major engagement. Furthermore, Johnston had been driven across the Oostanaula and the Federals were closer to strategically vital city of Atlanta. The cost of the Federal victories so far was some 4,000 men. The Confederates had lost around 3,000 men. Since Johnston was badly lacking in manpower and had little chance of finding any significant reinforcements, this loss was a serious blow to the Army of Tennessee. Still, Johnston had successfully evaded all of Sherman's attempts to fulfill his directives to entrap and destroy the Confederate command. The Army of Tennessee was still quite a formidable fighting force which could delay and even defeat Sherman if the opportunity presented itself.

CHAPTER V

TRAP AT CASSVILLE

16 May - 20 May, 1864

After losing Resaca, Johnston had some difficulty finding suitable ground to block Sherman's columns as they snaked their way south in pursuit of the Army of Tennessee. The area from the Oostanaula south to the Etowah River was open terrain with few geographical features to assist in the defense of an army. With no natural barriers to anchor flanks or contribute to a defense, the Army of Tennessee was especially vulnerable to Sherman's larger numbers which could easily maneuver to encircle and

Previous page: Sherman's army passes through Resaca on 15 May 1864 in pursuit of Johnston's Army of Tennessee after the Confederate retreated from defensive positions before the city and headed south.

crush them. Johnston's only option north of the Etowah was to hesitate and retreat until his enemy made a mistake, or better ground was found.

Johnston's defensive postures and Fabian reluctance to offer battle, along with Sherman's tenacious advances, formed a pattern that was played out over and over again through the months of May, June and July. First, Johnston found a strong position, fortified it and attempted to block his enemy's advance. Sherman responded by occupying Johnston's front line while seeking to maneuver around one of the Confederate flanks. These actions compelled Johnston to fall back once more, in search of a new location to form a defense, and the game began all over again. This relatively bloodless ritual was repeated with an almost formal regularity as the armies moved south of the Oostanaula.

On 16 May, Johnston fell back along the Western & Atlantic Railroad to the valley of the Oothcaloga Creek, near Calhoun. His stay there would be short. Finding the terrain in the valley untenable, Johnston retreated to a seemingly more advantageous site near Adairsville the next day. Sherman quickly pursued, after audaciously dividing his command in the hope of somehow pinning Johnston down north of the Etowah where the Confederates were at a clear disadvantage. The National forces drove south from the Oostanaula with Thomas' army taking the center, the *Army of the Tennessee* on his right and the *Army of the Ohio* on his left. As the Federal armies marched deeper into the interior of Georgia, some Yankees found the Peach State to their liking. One soldier wrote, "Georgia is indeed the Yankee state of the South. There is an appearance of neatness and comfort about the farm houses and residences of the poorer classes much resembling the North...."

However, the National troops found their appreciation of the countryside marred by their relentless Confederate adversary. As the Yankees advanced on Johnston's position outside of Adairsville, the Federals encountered Rebel skirmishers shielded by breastworks of logs and rails. When the Southerners were rooted from their cover by sharp fighting, they would merely retreat to another position prepared in the rear. Despite this stiff resistance, Sherman's army reached Johnston's front by the afternoon of 17 May.

By falling back to Adairsville, Johnston hoped to fight Sherman on low ridges north of the town. Once there, the Confederate general found a gap in the heights much too wide to be effectively defended. Johnston felt he had no choice but to fall back even further. After Major General B. F. Cheatham's division fought a bloody holding action, the rest of the Army of Tennessee headed south on the night of 17 May.

The town of Adairsville, Georgia. Johnston briefly attempted to hold Sherman's army outside of Adairsville on 17 May, but retreated further south after he found his position there untenable.

William J. Hardee
1815-1873

William J. Hardee is universally remembered as a Civil War commander of solid and dependable, though unremarkable, fighting ability which won him the name of "Old Reliable." After graduating from West Point in 1838, Hardee enjoyed an active military career before fighting for his native Georgia in the Civil War. His résumé included action with the Second Dragoons, two years on the western frontier, and a period studying of cavalry tactics at Saumur, France. He attained battle experience fighting in the National army against the Seminoles and served with distinction under Zachary Taylor and Winfield Scott during the Mexican War, where he won two brevets. Following the Mexican War, Hardee attained the ranks of major and then lieutenant colonel as well as the post of Commandant of Cadets at West Point, 1856-1861. Probably his most notable act was to write a manual of field tactics which was subsequently used by both sides during the Civil War.

Hardee advanced quickly after he joined the Confederate military, receiving a commission as a colonel when he entered the service, a brigadier generalcy

Lieutenant General William J. Hardee

in June of 1861, and the rank of major general by October of that year. Hardee saw action in many of the great battles out West, under the leadership of Albert Sidney Johnston and Braxton Bragg in the Army of Tennessee. After his service at the battle of Perryville, Kentucky on 8 October 1862, he was promoted to lieutenant general. Maintaining a distrust and dislike for Bragg, Hardee, along with Leonidas Polk, was one of the leading conspirators against the general during his unhappy tenure of command of the Army of Tennessee. After Bragg's resignation in November of 1863, Hardee temporarily assumed control of the Army of Tennessee, but refused President Jefferson Davis' requests to take permanent command.

During the Atlanta campaign, Hardee led most of Hood's ill-conceived attacks against Sherman in July and August. Hood blamed Hardee for the losses, thus causing the relationship between the two generals to deteriorate, and Hardee to demand a transfer. After the Atlanta campaign, Hardee was given command of the Department of South Carolina and attempted to field Sherman's advance to Savannah and into the Carolinas, without much success. His forces were merged with Johnston's command during the final weeks of the war and surrendered with them in mid-April.

After the war, Hardee lived out his last few years in peace and quiet in Alabama.

This time, Johnston retreated with confidence. On the night of the seventeenth, he had devised an ambitious plan to take advantage of Sherman's increasingly predictable advances. The crafty general's designs rested on the fact that two roads led from Adairsville to Cassville; one route led southeast directly to the town, while another followed the Western & Atlantic as it trailed off ten miles south to Kingston and then proceeded six miles east to Cassville. Johnston anticipated that Sherman would divide his forces yet again to take advantage of the roads and trap the Confederate army at Kingston by sending part of his force to Cassville. In order to benefit from this move, Johnston divided his forces as well to launch a trap of his own. To give the Federals the impression that Kingston was the destination of the Army of Tennessee, Hardee moved there with Wheeler's cavalry and the Confederate wagon train. Meanwhile, Hood's and Polk's corps marched southeast for Cassville to wait for, entrap and

Gone With the Wind: A Civil War Saga of Print and Film

Perhaps the most common association which the Atlanta campaign has in the minds of people today is with Margaret Mitchell's massive epic, *Gone With the Wind*, and the cinematic masterpiece of the same name which it inspired. Since the publication of *Gone with the Wind* in 1937, the book has become an international best seller; millions have thrilled to the ambition, guiles and will of its heroine, Scarlett O'Hara. The book, and even the movie, is one of the best fictional representations of the idyllic myth of the old South destroyed by Yankee depredations in war and Reconstruction and its struggle to attain rebirth.

Author Margaret Mitchell was born in Atlanta, the city she would become closely identified with, in 1900, to Eugene and Maybelle Stephens Mitchell. Her father was a prominent lawyer as well as president of the Atlanta Historical Society. While her parents were born after the war and did not suffer the supposed ill effects of Reconstruction, she grew up in an atmosphere propagating the Civil War as the famed "Lost Cause." This idealism depicted a South of wealth, power and a genteel lifestyle, destroyed by Yankee oppression despite the efforts of courageous white males, sacrificing belles, and loyal Negro slaves.

Mitchell left Georgia in 1918 to attend college, ironically, in the North at Smith College in Northampton, Massachusetts. She became engaged, but lost her lover to the fighting in France during World War I. After Mitchell's mother died in 1919, she returned to Atlanta to care for her father and brother and manage her old home. From 1922 to 1926, she worked for the *Atlanta Journal*, writing over 129 articles for the *Atlanta Journal Sunday Magazine*, including a series on Georgia's Confederate generals. Mitchell married a lecherous individual by the name of Barrien K. "Red" Upshaw in 1922. Upshaw abused and finally left her allowing the marriage to lapse into divorce. In 1925, Mitchell married again this time to a more reputable fellow by the name of John R. Marsh, who had served as her first husband's best man. She would live happily with Marsh for the rest of her life.

Mitchell resigned from the *Atlanta Journal* after suffering an ankle injury. Her husband then encouraged her to start writing a book which she did with a vengeance. Having written the concluding chapter first, it took ten years for Mitchell to complete the rest of a work of historical fiction entitled *Tomorrow is Another Day*, which featured a Southern heroine named Pansy.

In the spring of 1935, Mitchell was to meet with Harold S. Latham who was traveling the country for the Macmillan publishing company searching for marketable manuscripts. Friends who knew of Mitchell's work prodded her to submit her manuscript, but the author demurred, arguing that a Northern publisher would have little interest in a book with a Southern perspective on the Civil War. Eventually, Mitchell acquiesced and turned over a massive five foot-pile of typescript. When Macmillan accepted the book, Mitchell meticulously edited her work to check for any historical inaccuracies and verify dates, places and other details. The 1,035 page book sporting 460,000 words, with the altered title of *Gone with the Wind,* finally appeared on 30 June 1936.

Mitchell described her work thusly, "It is basically just a simple yarn of fairly simple people. There's no fine writing, there are no grandiose thoughts, no symbolism, nothing sensational...." The story details the trials and tribulations of four main characters: the ambitious Scarlet O'Hara, the roguish Rhett Butler, the chivalrous Ashley Wilkes and Melanie Hamilton, a fragile belle. The story takes place throughout the Civil War and Reconstruction periods and serves as a compendium of the Southern lore and life of that era.

The book received sensational acclaim from critics and readers. Most reviewers praised the work and author, while others attacked it as racist trash. The public flocked to bookstores, and 50,000 copies were bought up in the first day, 1 million were sold in sixth months, and the book topped sales of 2 million in a year. Mitchell was also to win the Pulitzer Prize and the American Bookseller's Award in 1937.

However, Mitchell was uncomfortable with the instant popularity that her "simple yarn" had created; she never wrote another novel. Though she did sign a contract with David O. Selznick for the film rights, she refused to participate in the making of the film. In 1949, Mitchell's life was brought to an untimely end when she was struck by a car on 11 August and died five days later.

Mitchell's mammoth novel has been one of the largest selling publications in American history. Millions of copies have been sold in this country and around the world. The book has been translated into 30 languages and can be found in at least

40 countries. Despite the overwhelming popularity of the novel, perhaps its greatest and most remembered bequest is the epic movie of the same name.

The story behind the production of *Gone with the Wind* is almost as fascinating as the epic yarn depicted on the screen. At first, Hollywood was loathe to touch the daunting chores of bringing the book to screen. Though Mitchell's work was a best seller, the consensus in the film industry was that no money could be made off of a motion picture on the Civil War. However, David O. Selznick of Selznick International was eventually convinced to buy permission to make a film out of the book for $30,000, the highest amount ever paid for movie rights up to that time.

Once Selznick was committed to the project, he ensured that he got the perfect cast. For the part of Rhett Butler, Selznick envisioned Clark Gable. Though Gable was hardly enthused with the chance to play Butler, he accepted the part for a hefty sum of $100,000. Selznick had British actor Leslie Howard in mind for the role of languid Ashley Wilkes. Like Gable, Howard was not too eager to play his assigned character in *Gone With the Wind*. Though he considered the Wilkes character weak, watery and ineffectual, Howard eventually agreed after Selznick promised him a large salary and the position of associate producer on another film. For the part of Melanie Hamilton, Selznick seized upon the idea of using Olivia de Havilland. However, de Havilland was contracted to Warner Brothers. When Jack Warner was approached for permission to use the actress in *Gone With the Wind*, he demanded Selznick engage other Warner Brothers stars in leading roles as part of the bargain. Warner visualized Errol Flynn playing the part of Butler and Bette Davis as Scarlett O'Hara. Unlike Gable and Howard, de Havilland was eager for a part in the movie. Fortunately, she was a good friend of Warner's wife, who was able to convince the mogul to lend the actress out to Selznick with no strings attached.

These difficulties in lining up actors for the roles of Butler, Wilkes and Hamilton dwarfed the difficulties Selznick faced in attempting to find just the right actress to play the role of Scarlett O'Hara. The hunt turned into a major publicity event and diverted public attention from "less important" events in Europe and Asia. For over two years, Selznick scoured the country to find the perfect woman for the part. Over 2,000 women auditioned, among them such notables as Joan Crawford, Jean Harlow, Ann Sheridan, Carole Lombard, Claudette Colbert, Irene Dunne, Tallulah Bankhead, Lana Turner, and even Lucille Ball. Hundreds hopeful unknowns also tried out and fought for the chance to play Scarlett. Some desperate would be actresses followed and pestered Selznick and one even "mailed" herself to his office. Though Selznick was frustrated in his search, filming began with the famous burning of Atlanta. While viewing the project, Selznick met two guests of his talent agent brother, Myron Selznick: actor Laurence Olivier and his fiancee, actress Vivian Leigh. Myron introduced Leigh by jokingly exclaiming, "Here, genius, I want you to meet Scarlett O'Hara!" Selznick took one look at Leigh and decided she was the woman for the part. Leigh was taken in for a screen test and hired to play the role.

Another massive difficulty Selznick faced was the script for the movie. The book *Gone with the Wind* had developed a huge cult-like following that would be hanging on every word of the movie. If everything was not done completely right for these demanding fans, Selznick would have hell to pay. A number of writers were employed to write the text, working directly from the book. Among them was F. Scott Fitzgerald, who had fallen on hard times and was working for Hollywood to make extra money. Despite Fitzgerald's fame, and the many other writers who had worked on the script, only one, Sidney Howard was mentioned in the credits.

The film was first directed by George Cukor, who was later replaced by Victor Fleming at Clark Gable's request. Fleming was an action director who won ever lasting fame for his direction of the classic *Wizard of Oz*. Fleming threw his heart and soul into the project. His herculean efforts drove him to depression and even to contemplate suicide. He finally suffered a nervous breakdown and had to be taken to a hospital for rest while another director was called in to work on some scenes.

Filming began in late 1938 and was completed after 140 days of work at a cost of $4,250,000. The film premiered before a sold out audience of 2,051 people in the Grand Theater at Atlanta almost a year later on 15 December 1939. Outside, a gargantuan crowd of one million people gathered to get a glimpse at the celebrities in attendance that night. As the movie opened around the country and the world, millions bought tickets to see the spectacle in 1939, and for years to come. By 1943, it had grossed $32,000,000, by 1959 it had made $50,000,000 around the world, $70,000,000 by 1967 and $79,000,000 by 1989.

Though *Gone With the Wind* has often been criticized as racist and meandering in old myths of the South and the "Lost Cause," it remains a classic. Aspects of both the book and the film have left their indelible imprint on American culture and continue to inspire readers and movie goers in a fashion unrivaled by any other work historical fiction.

destroy the exposed Federal column moving on the town from Adairsville. If all went as planned, the Federals would suffer a devastating defeat.

Sherman acted precisely as Johnston had predicted. The Federal general was intensely eager to catch the Army of Tennessee north of the Etowah and jumped at the chance to catch the Rebels at Kingston. Ignoring caution, Sherman divided his forces on 18 May; the *Army of the Tennessee* and the *Army of the Cumberland* were sent towards Kingston, while the *Army of the Ohio* with Hooker's XX Corps were dispatched to Cassville. The armies marched on 18-19 May with Schofield's and Hooker's troops unknowingly advancing into the jaws of a potentially disastrous situation.

With all going according to plan on 19 May, Johnston jubilantly declared in an address to his troops that the army would retreat no further:

> Soldiers of the Army of Tennessee, you have displayed the highest quality of the soldier—firmness in combat, patience under toil. By your courage and skill you have repulsed every assault of the enemy. By marches by day and by marches by night you have defeated every attempt upon your communications....You will now turn and march to meet his advancing columns. Fully confiding in the conduct of the officers, the courage of the soldiers, I lead you to battle. We may confidently trust that the Almighty Father will still reward the patriots' toils and bless the patriots' banners.

The Confederate commander had an additional reason to be confident in his chance of victory; the last of his reinforcements from Polk's Army of Mississippi had arrived to join the Army of Tennessee, bringing its troop strength up to some 70,000 men.

On the morning of 19 May, the trap began to close as the Confederates moved out of their entrenchments to hit Schofield's and Hooker's exposed forces outside of Cassville. Johnston's plan detailed Hood's Corps to attack the Federal left flank, Polk to assail the center, and Hardee to withdraw from Kingston to deal a blow against the Federal right. Despite the unparalleled opportunity, the Confederate plan somehow misfired. Hood advanced up a country road to get on the National left, only to find what he assumed to be a strong enemy force on his right. In actuality the force was merely some cavalry and a lost detachment of befuddled infantry, but Hood considered the threat serious enough to cancel his attack. Hood's chief of staff reported the encountered menace to Johnston, and the corps retreated to take up position next to Polk. Seeing his attempt to launch an offensive collapse, Johnston decided at 1600 to pull his entire army back to a better defensive position on a 140-foot wooded ridge to the southeast of Cassville.

Johnston and Hood would later argue about the responsibility for the Confederate failure to launch an attack on 19 May. Johnston argued that Hood had panicked unnecessarily and hadn't even bothered to investigate the negligible force on his right. For his part, Hood claimed that Johnston had made no grand plans for an attack at Cassville. Instead, Hood himself had asked his commander to move forward on his own initiative, only to retreat when the Federals were found on his flank. Whatever the cause, Schofield and Hooker escaped harm, and a great opportunity was lost.

By mid-day on the nineteenth, Sherman became aware that his army was in danger. The *Army of the Tennessee* and the *Army of the Cumberland* began arriving at Kingston at 0800 to find only light resistance instead of the Army of Tennessee. At first, the befuddled Sherman assumed from the disappearance of most of Johnston's force that the enemy was retreating for the Etowah. By 1200, he had become aware of and responded to the Confederate concentration against Schofield at Cassville. He quickly set Thomas' and McPherson's armies in motion to follow the retreating Hardee east, and the rest of the Federal troops arrived before Cassville during the late afternoon and evening of the nineteenth. With the Confederates seemingly ready to make a stand, Sherman prepared his troops for a major battle.

Though Johnston's attempt at an offensive had failed, the general was supremely confident that his new line south of Cassville could withstand a Federal attack. However, the Confederate general soon found, to his extreme discomfiture, that while his defensive position appeared strong, it actually contained a potentially critical weakness. The four-mile Confederate line was drawn up along a ridge with Hood on the right, Polk in the center and Hardee on the left. After Sherman's troops began to form before the Army of Tennessee, a threat to a section of Polk's line held by Major General Samuel G. French's Division became evident. Once Federal artillery opened fire on French's men, their position proved to be particularly vulnerable to cannon fire. Yankee batteries blasted apart Rebel field pieces with well-placed counter battery fire while Southern troops were forced to scramble for cover under a deadly rain of shells. Hood and Polk learned of French's situation and both came to the conclusion that the position could not be held for long under such a destructive fire.

The path of the Western & Atlantic Railroad through Allatoona Pass. Johnston held the pass in May with the Army of Tennessee. Several months later, it would be held by Major General John M. Corse and his division of Federals against an attack by John B. Hood as he fell on Sherman's communications in north Georgia.

During a conference on the night of the nineteenth, Johnston learned from Polk and Hood that the Cassville line was untenable. According to Johnston, when he met with the two corps commanders that evening, both heatedly argued that the only course available to the army was to retreat south of the Etowah. However, Hood later claimed that he and Polk actually asked Johnston to advance against the Federal army to drive off their guns, rather than ignominiously fall back. In any case, Johnston was uncertain about the viability of conducting a defense at Cassville over the objections of two of his corps commanders. When Hardee appeared on the scene, he vociferously objected to the idea of another retreat, but his superior ignored his counsel. Though Johnston professed his continued faith in the Cassville position, he was reluctant to make a stand before the Federal army without the confidence of Polk and Hood. Thus, his only option appeared to be to fall back across the Etowah.

On the night of the nineteenth, the same day as Johnston's famous stand and fight order, the soldiers of the Army of Tennessee received word of the retreat. Johnston abandoned his lines and moved to a new position in the Allatoona Pass south of the Etowah, where the Western & Atlantic passed through a rugged range.

Finding that the Confederates had disappeared from his front a third time, Sherman decided to rest his forces at Kingston and Cassville before advancing forward once more. The Western & Atlantic was repaired to allow supplies to move forward into the new Federal camps. Oscar L. Jackson, an officer of the *63d Ohio*, wrote of the railroad on 20 May, ."..we have cars running to Kingston today. Only those who belong to the army know how encouraging the sound of the locomotive is, for by it we get our supplies of all kinds."

With Johnston occupying a tough set of hills across the Etowah, Sherman was once again faced with the Army of Tennessee in a strong position, defying the Federal advance. However, the Federal general had another daring plan in mind. To get on the flank and in the rear of his adversary he would boldly leave his own supply line and entirely circumvent the Confederate army.

CHAPTER VI

HELL HOLE

23 May - 6 June, 1864

As Sherman rested his army at Kingston and Cassville from 20-23 May, he planned the next audacious phase of his operations. Knowing that Johnston's position across the Etowah was much too strong to attack directly, Sherman decided to continue his successful strategy of turning the enemy's flank. To do so, Sherman intended to send his forces against Dallas, around 14 miles south of the Etowah. From there, they would head 20 miles to the east for the Western & Atlantic Railroad at Marietta. Back in 1844, when Sherman was a lieutenant in the Third Artillery, he had been briefly stationed in Georgia and had traveled over the ground of his future Atlanta campaign. Sherman's knowledge of the area gave him a good idea of the risks his movement might involve. Though the ground about Dallas was ill suited to extensive campaigning, Sherman was confident that he could successfully move through the rough countryside and into the enemy rear. Despite Sherman's optimism, there was much that could possibly hinder and even endanger his troops as they made the proposed movement. Only a few poor roads provided the army with routes through the sharp ravines, dense pine forests and ponds of quicksand covering that section of Georgia. Worse still, a move on Dallas would entail Sherman's abandonment of his supply line of the Western & Atlantic Railroad, forcing his troops to survive off of supplies carried with the army or whatever could be gleaned from the inhospitable countryside. However, Sherman believed the probable gains would outweigh any potential risks. If the mission were successful, Johnston might be compelled to fall back from his secure position at the Allatoona Pass, possibly all the way to the Chattahoochee River north of Atlanta. Sherman confidently wrote Chief of Staff Major General Henry W. Halleck of his plans on 21 May. "I allow three days to have the army grouped about Dallas, whence I can strike at Marietta, or the Chattahoochee, according to developments. You may not hear from us in some days, but be assured we are not idle or thoughtless."

On 23 May, Sherman had his army cross the Etowah west of the Allatoona Pass and move forward in three columns. Thomas once again took the center, moving south from Kingston through Stilesboro. Schofield took the eastern most route through

62 / THE ATLANTA CAMPAIGN

Burnt Hickory, in supporting distance of the *Army of the Cumberland*'s left. McPherson's *Army of the Tennessee* took a wide turn out to the southwest through Van Wert before moving back to the east to rejoin the rest of the army. Cavalry covered the flanks and rear of the army while the whole force was in motion. "The Etowah is the Rubicon of Georgia," Sherman wrote in his diary. "We are now all in motion like a vast hive of bees, and expect to swarm along the Chattahoochee in a few days."

It didn't take long for Johnston to fathom Sherman's intentions. On 23 May, Rebel cavalry reported that the Federals were active and on the move. On that day, Johnston took the precaution of shifting Polk and Hardee out to the west towards Dallas. By the next day, the Confederate commander was sure that Dallas was the Federal objective and ordered a concentration near the town to block the enemy advance. By 25 May, the Southerners were in position outside of Dallas, with Hood holding the right four miles northeast of the town, near a small Methodist meeting house known as the New Hope Church. Polk and Hardee were on his left. The Confederates were once again in terrain advantageous for a defensive stand, with their troops well entrenched on a wooded ridge and set up to block the roads from Dallas to Marietta

View of Allatoona Gap. Johnston's formidable defensive position at Allatoona effected Sherman's decision to flank the Confederates by moving on Dallas.

and Atlanta.

As the Federals advanced on Dallas, Sherman quickly discovered that his offensive was not going according to plan. Increasingly, the Federals were finding that Johnston was competently countering to their moves. On the twenty-fourth, the Federals started running into stiff Confederate resistance. That same day, Sherman received a captured Confederate dispatch which informed him that the Confederates were moving on Dallas. It appeared as though Sherman's troops were advancing towards a major confrontation with the enemy, not the Chattahoochee.

The next day, Hooker's command, in advance of Thomas' *Army of the Cumberland*, encountered the Rebels in force near Dallas. After crossing the Pumpkin Vine Creek around 1000, Geary's division of the *XX Corps* ran into fire from Confederate skirmishers. After learning from captured Southerners that a large enemy force was nearby, Geary met with Hooker and Thomas to discuss the uncertain situation. Rather than launching an ill-considered attack, Hooker ordered the rest of his divisions to join Geary while Thomas had his two other corps move forward towards the area as well. When Sherman joined his subordinates, he believed Hooker to be on

64 / THE ATLANTA CAMPAIGN

Map of action from Adairsville to Dallas.

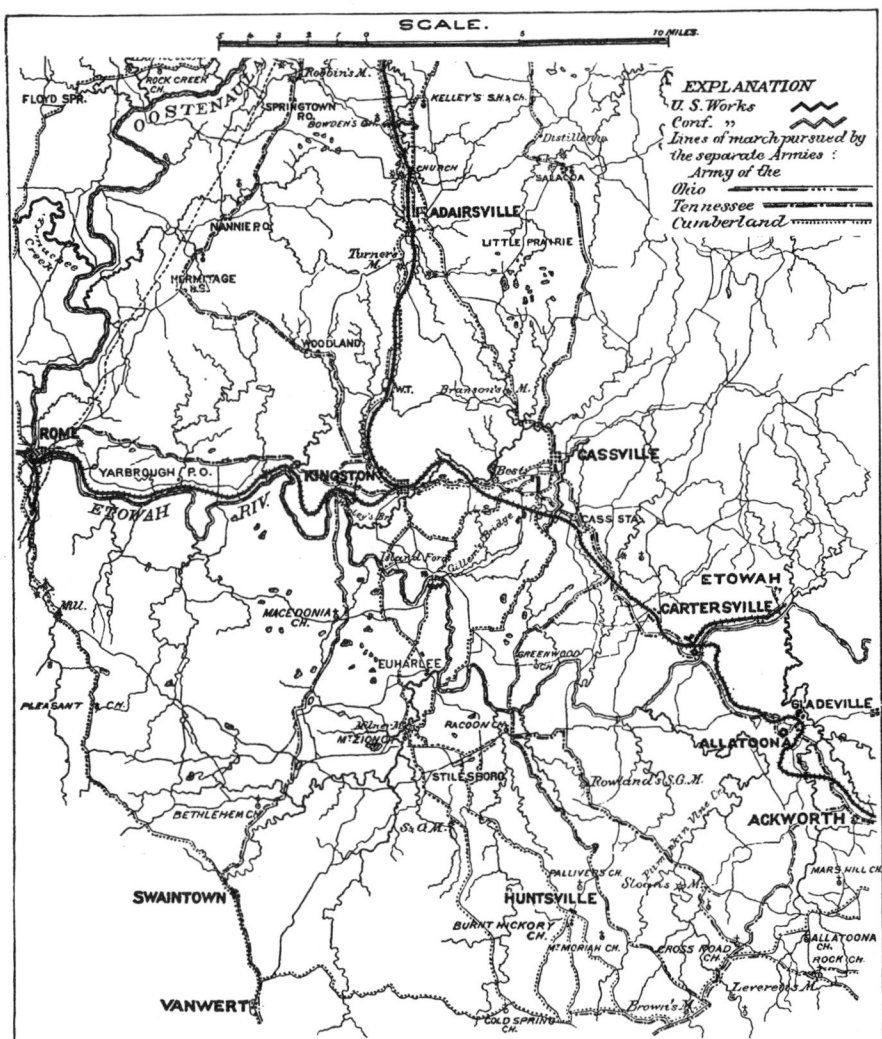

the left flank of the Confederate line and contemplated ordering an immediate attack. However, Thomas and Hooker convinced him to wait at least until the rest of the *XX Corps* could be brought up to support Geary. Still, Sherman refused to believe that any major threat existed in front of Hooker. "I don't see what they are waiting for right now. There haven't been more than twenty rebels there today," he told one of Thomas' staff officers. The poor roads and rough terrain delayed the rest of Hooker's corps from reaching the field and launching the Federal attack. It wasn't until 1600 that the Federals were finally on the move against the Confederate right occupied by Hood.

Hood's divisions were set up with A. P. Stewart in the center, Thomas Hindman on the left and C. L. Stevenson on the right. Stewart occupied the best position on a piece of high ground near the New Hope Church, with his line solidly bolstered by 16 pieces of artillery. The Southerners had spent most of the day preparing to meet the impending Federal advance. Troops diligently dug trenches and constructed breastworks of rails, logs and sticks, while the area in front of their line was cleared to provide an open field of fire. The Confederate reception of the coming attack would prove to be a harsh one.

In preparing for his attack, Hooker placed Williams' division on his right and Geary's on his left, while Major General Daniel Butterfield's division was kept in reserve. The divisions were massed in columns of brigades, a formation intended to concentrate the maximum amount of force in order to smash through the enemy line.

When a halt is ordered, Federals relax, eat and drink after an arduous march. Sherman's troops were forced to negotiate over harsh terrain made worse by an almost constant rain as they advanced into Georgia in May and June.

However, in the case of the fight at New Hope Church, it proved to be a costly mistake. Though the Federal corps heavily outnumbered Stewart, the unit was formed in such a way that it could not take advantage of its superior numbers to flank the enemy position. In fact, the total width of the combined attacking divisions of the *XX Corps* was just about the same as that of Stewart's Division, making the Federal advance a full frontal assault into the destructive firepower of a well-entrenched enemy.

The Federals plowed forward just as a brewing thunderstorm covered the sky in a grey shroud of darkness. One observer remarked of the Federal troops during the advance, "One would think these fine fellows were going to a parade, instead of death, so calm and composed did they look." The National troops moved through a dense thicket until they came upon a parapet of logs and red earth "blazing with fire and death" in the words of one participant.

Undaunted, the Yankees pressed forward into vollies of musketry and devastating blasts of shells and canister from enemy cannons. Geary wrote in his report of the battle, "The discharges of canister and shell from the enemy were heavier than in any other battle of the campaign in which my command were engaged." One soldier remembered of the fire that day, "The canister and case shot in particular, hissed, swished, and sung around and among us...ripping up the ground, throwing dirt up in our faces and rolling at our feet, until those who were not hit by them were ready to conclude that they surely would be hit." When the *125th New York* lay down to seek cover from the fire, another regiment advanced over the troops of the Excelsior

Joseph Hooker
1814-1879

Throughout the annals of the history of the *Army of the Potomac*, there are a series of tragic figures; commanders who might have been great heroes and forever lionized in American history, but who for one reason or another suffered disastrous failure and now remain mere sidenotes in the national memory. Members of this dishonored group include George Brinton McClellan, Ambrose Burnside and, perhaps the most tragic of all, Joseph Hooker.

Hooker was a Massachusetts man who was educated in local schools and went on to graduate from West Point, ranked twenty-ninth in the class of 1837. He displayed a great competence for combat which won him three brevets in the Mexican War. He was later detailed to California where he met his future commander in the Atlanta campaign, William Tecumseh Sherman. While serving out in California, Hooker took a two year leave of absence from 1851, and thereafter decided to resign from the army to take up farming. Hooker's endeavors yielded little by the way of success and prompted his attempt to re-enter the army in 1858. For some reason, his application was not acted upon and Hooker's future seemed doomed to obscurity.

Like many other of his fellow West Pointers who had fallen on hard times, the outbreak of the Civil War retrieved his fortunes. By August of 1861, Hooker was a brigadier general of the volunteers. At first, Hooker commanded a brigade detailed to protect the Federal capital of Washington, D.C., but then took to the field of battle leading a division of the *III Corps* during the Peninsular Campaign. At this time, the general won the nickname that he would carry throughout the war when a newspaper misread a Federal dispatch which ran "Fighting—Joe Hooker" and created the sobriquet, "Fighting Joe."

Major General Joseph Hooker

Hooker's star rose steadily after the Peninsular campaign. He was promoted to major general, given corps command and led a smashing, but doomed attack at Antietam, where he was mildly wounded. The general recovered to lead several corps in the disaster at Fredericksburg. After the battle, Hooker severely criticized his superior Major General Ambrose Burnside, who was later relieved. This event opened the way for the dashing and ambitious Hooker to take command of the *Army of the Potomac*. Hooker's reputation as a hard fighter, as well as his connections with Secretary of the Treasury Salmon P. Chase, sealed his appointment to the command. Lincoln seemed to have reservations about the general, due to the latter's foolish claim that a dictator might have to be appointed if the war was to be won. The president calmly told Hooker that he would risk dictatorship if the general would win battles.

At first, Hooker showed promise as an army commander by restoring the confidence of a demoralized *Army of the Potomac* and the creation of a daring plan to defeat Confederate mastermind Robert E. Lee which just might have worked. However, Hooker failed to execute his designs correctly and was humiliatingly defeated by Lee at the battle of Chancellorsville. As a result of his confusion during the early days of the Gettysburg campaign, Lincoln removed "Fighting Joe" and replaced him with Major General George Gordon Meade.

Hooker soon returned to field command, leading two corps sent west to help relieve the *Army of the Cumberland*, besieged at Chattanooga. There, he managed to win a major victory at Lookout Mountain. By 1864, his two corps were consolidated into one, named the *XX Corps* and assigned to the *Army of the Cumberland* during the Atlanta campaign. Though Hooker performed fairly ably throughout the advance into Georgia, he ran afoul of Sherman. The animosity between these two men exploded when Sherman refused even to consider "Fighting Joe" for the vacancy at the head of the *Army of the Tennessee* created by the death of James B. McPherson. To add insult to injury, Sherman actually appointed a junior to Hooker, Oliver O. Howard. The disgusted Hooker asked to be relieved and saw no further service during the war. He attempted to stir up trouble for Sherman by criticizing his former commander's ability and arguing that he should be labeled insane. Hooker's efforts came to naught in the wake of Sherman's stunning victories, which won the respect of a grateful Union.

Hooker retired from the service in 1868 and died more than ten years later. He was an able divisional and corps leader, but when confronted with army command, he lost his nerve when he needed it most. Hooker is probably best remembered today through a dubious Civil War legend which links his surname to ladies of ill repute: "hookers."

State, only to meet a baleful discharge of artillery. Lieutenant James C. Rogers wrote of the incident,

> ...scarcely had it formed in front when the enemy's battery which had been silent for a few minutes, opened again, and this gallant relief, unable to appreciate so warm a reception, rushed in disorder to the rear, all attempts to stop them and force them back to their place, even with a line of bayonets, proving useless.

The Confederates were remembered as firing with a professional "steadiness and firmness." A Confederate recalled that the enemy advanced like a surging wave which all but vanished when the Confederates' "angry rifles spat their fire and hungry cannon belched their flame." Stewart remained in the thick of the battle, riding the Confederate line and ignoring the pleas of his troops that he seek cover. When a concerned Johnston sent a dispatch to inquire if Stewart needed any reinforcements, the general nonchalantly replied, "My own troops will hold this position."

The Yankees made several attempts to drive the enemy troops from their works, but each effort met with failure and heavy casualties. Defeated, Hooker's troops fell back as a thunderstorm pounded the carnage left behind on the battlefield. The *XX Corps* suffered around 1,800 casualties in its futile attacks against the Confederate works at New Hope Church. A soldier in Stewart's command wrote that the battlefield where the Federals had been slaughtered seemed like a "seething mass of quivering flesh." There are no accurate numbers for Confederate losses, but they were presumably minimal.

William T. Sherman during his campaign against the Confederate line at Dallas.

Rebel entrenchments used by Cheatham's men to repel Sherman's assault at New Hope Church. As the battle raged, Major General Cheatham remained on the front lines to share the danger of his men.

After the failure of the attack at New Hope Church, Sherman began to concentrate the rest of his army near Dallas. Thomas brought the *Army of the Cumberland* up to join Hooker at New Hope Church, McPherson's troops arrived to take a position two miles in advance of Dallas, and Schofield took the left flank north of Thomas. Cavalry guarded both flanks from any surprise attack. Johnston himself reorganized his line slightly on 26 May. Realizing that the Federals were strongest near New Hope Church, Johnston made preparations to strengthen the right of his line there. Hood shifted Hindman from the left to the north and Cleburne's division of Hardee's Corps was sent to Hood's right to extend the Confederate flank even further.

On the twenty-sixth, soldiers of both sides squared off against each other. Both Confederates and Federals took time to strengthen their positions with dirt, logs and fence rails to find protection from the constant and intense picket fire from enemy troops nearby. In some places, the Confederate and Federal skirmishers were so close to each other that the advance guard could only be changed safely in the darkness of night.

There was almost no way to find protection from the weather. Troops were forced to suffer through unbearably thick mugginess when the stifling Georgia heat mixed with the rains to turn the woods around Dallas into a sultry jungle. It is little wonder that the position became known as the "Hell-Hole."

Though Sherman found the enemy line a tough nut to crack on 25 May, he decided to launch an assault meant to turn Johnston's right flank on the twenty-seventh. Howard was to lead the assault with Brigadier General Thomas J. Wood's division of the *IV Corps* of the *Army of the Cumberland*, supported by Brigadier General Richard W. Johnson's division of the *XIV Corps* and Nathaniel C. McLean's brigade from the *Army of the Ohio*. All together, some 14,000 men would be involved in the maneuver. To increase the chance of success, an artillery barrage would precede the attack, and the rest of the Federal army would distract Johnston by making demonstrations against other parts of the Rebel position.

On the morning of 27 May, Wood's troops were pulled out of the main line, followed by Johnson's division, and marched east through the dense woods over treacherous ravines and ridges. With much difficulty, Howard's force managed to find the Confederate flank around 1500, where Cleburne's men were busy fortifying their new position two miles northeast of New Hope Church close to the small community of Picket's Mill.

Cleburne had uncovered the Federal movement and his troops were preparing a harsh welcome for the enemy advance by strengthening the Confederate right. The Irish born Confederate extended the flank with Brigadier General Hiram D. Granbury's brigade of Texans. Some 1,000 men of John H. Kelly's cavalry were dismounted and posted on the extreme right. Twelve guns of Hotchkiss' battery were placed on Cleburne's front so as to gain a deadly enfilade on the Federals when they moved forward.

Meanwhile, the Yankees were preparing an onslaught that was doomed to falter. Howard decided to mass Wood's division in a column of brigades, the very tactic which had proved ineffectual at New Hope Church just a few days earlier. Brigadier General William B. Hazen's brigade was to advance first, followed by Colonel William H. Gibson's men, and then Colonel Frederick Knefler's command. Wood's men were to receive support on the left from Colonel Benjamin Scribner's brigade of Johnson's division and McLean's brigade on the right. Just before the attack, Wood turned to Howard and said, "We will put in Hazen and see what success he has." The remark convey conveyed little hope or enthusiasm to the commander who would lead the first assault. One of Hazen's staff officers, future novelist Ambrose Bierce, later recorded Hazen's reaction to Wood's careless statement in a bitter article entitled "The Crime at Pickett's Mill":

> ...when he heard Wood say they would put him in and see what success he would have in defeating an army—when he saw Howard assent—he uttered never a word, rode to the head of his feeble brigade and patiently awaited the command to go. Only by a look which I knew how to read did he betray his sense of the criminal blunder.

It was 1630 by the time the attack got underway. At 1635, Howard penned a message to Thomas stating that his troops were on the move, "I...am now turning the enemy's right, I think." The Federal charge quickly degenerated into a "criminally" confused affair. While Hazen's troops assaulted the Confederate line, its supporting units either got distracted or failed to advance. On Hazen's left, Scribner was pep-

A set defensive works built at New Hope Church by the Confederates to resist Sherman's advance.

pered with an annoying series of fusillades from Kelly's dismounted cavalry and paused to give them battle. On the right, McLean failed to incite his troops to make their presence felt at all during the fight. Meanwhile Gibson's brigade was dilatory about getting into position to support Hazen when that commander was engaged with the enemy. Hazen's assault was doomed at the outset, but his men, oblivious to the blunders being committed, advanced against the Rebel line, their ranks becoming increasingly disorganized in the tangled wood before the Confederate position. Bierce described the advance:

> We moved forward. In less than one minute the trim battalions had become simply a swarm of men struggling through the undergrowth of the forest, pushing and crowding. The front was irregularly serrated, the strongest and the bravest in advance, the others following in fan-like formations, variable and inconstant, ever defining themselves anew....The color-bearers kept well to the front with their flags, closely furled, aslant backward over their shoulders. Displayed they would have been torn to rags by the boughs of the trees.

Once in front of Granbury's men, the brigade was torn apart by a vicious barrage of musketry and grapeshot. Bierce wrote of the fire:

> Suddenly there came a ringing rattle of musketry, the familiar hissing of bullets, and before us the interspaces of the forest were all blue with smoke. Hoarse, fierce yells broke out of a thousand throats. The forward fringe of brave hardy assailants was arrested in its mutable extensions; the edge of the swarm grew dense and clearly defined as the foremost halted, and the rest pressed forward to align themselves beside them, all firing. The uproar was deafening; the air was sibilant with streams and sheets

Patrick R. Cleburne
1828-1864

Patrick R. Cleburne certainly must be one of the most wrongly unrecognized tactical masterminds of the Confederate military. A man who was willing to put his cause and victory before concern for his own career, Cleburne has long been overshadowed by many lesser Confederate warriors.

Cleburne was born in Ireland and pursued a career in medicine before he turned to a military profession in the service of the queen. In 1849, he resigned from the British army and left Great Britain to seek his fortune in the United States. He eventually settled in Arkansas, where he studied law and became a somewhat successful lawyer.

When Arkansas left the Union, Cleburne sought to join in the defense of his adopted state. He organized a company of volunteers called the Yell Rifles, served as its captain, and assisted in the seizure of the Federal arsenal at Little Rock. From this auspicious start, Cleburne quickly scaled the ladder of the Confederate army, becoming the colonel of the 15th Arkansas, and later a brigadier general under Major General William J. Hardee.

Cleburne's first real experience of battle command was at Shiloh, where he participated in the rout of the Federals on the first day of fighting, 6 April 1862, and helped cover the Confederate retreat the next day. Cleburne later rose to the command of a small division which he led with great skill at the battle of Richmond, Kentucky in August of 1862. During that same battle, the Irish born

Major General Patrick R. Cleburne

Confederate fell was seriously wounded when a bullet struck his cheek. Cleburne soon returned to field command to participate in the culmination of Braxton Bragg's raid into Kentucky, at Perryville on 8 October 1862. Promoted to major general, he saw action at Stone's River and Chickamauga and covered the Army of Tennessee's retreat into Georgia after its disastrous rout at Chattanooga.

Though a promising candidate for corps command, Cleburne ruined his chances for advancement when he suggested a radical scheme to retrieve the declining fortunes of the Confederate war effort. His revolutionary proposal called for the emancipation of black slaves willing to fight in the service of the South. Cleburne was willing to stake his own career to prove the merits of emancipation by offering to train and lead a command of freed slaves himself. The idea did not go over well with some of Cleburne's compatriots, and it stained the general in the eyes of President Davis, who firmly ordered the matter suppressed.

Cleburne continued to fight for his cause even though his inferiors in ability passed over him to achieve corps and even army command. Throughout the Atlanta campaign, Cleburne led his division with distinction. At Picket's Mill, he oversaw the bloody repulse of a Federal attempt to turn the Army of Tennessee's left during the confrontation between Sherman's and Johnston's forces near Dallas. In November of 1864, Cleburne sacrificed his life to his adopted nation when he led a fruitless charge against a strong enemy position at Franklin, Tennessee. The general fell, dead, 50 yards from the Federal line, at the forefront of his troops.

Cleburne was one of only two Confederate major generals who were born in a foreign country. His superlative skill in commanding infantry won the nickname of "the Stonewall Jackson of the West." An intelligent and friendly officer, the Confederacy did him a great wrong by failing to recognize his ability and castigating him for his attempt to save his adopted country.

72 / THE ATLANTA CAMPAIGN

Sherman's lieutenants: Oliver O. Howard (left), William B. Hazen and John Logan (center). Howard and Hazen were involved in the bloddy defeat at Pickett's Mill.

of missiles. In the steady, unvarying roar of small-arms the frequent shock of the cannon was rather felt than heard, but gusts of grape which they blew into that populous wood were audible enough, screaming among the trees and cracking their stems and branches. We had, of course, no artillery to reply.

The Federals quickly took whatever cover they could find behind trees and stones, or anything else available. A few groups of Yankees pressed forward into the hail of fire to charge the enemy line only, to be shot down for their bravado, as Bierce later recorded:

> In any instances which have come under my observation, when hostile lines of infantry engage at close range and the assailants afterwards retire, there was a 'dead-line' beyond which no man advanced but to fall. Not a soul of them ever reached the enemy's front to be bayoneted or captured....I observed this phenomenon at Pickett's Mill. Standing at the right of the line I had an unobstructed view of the narrow, open space across which the two lines fought. It was dim with smoke, but not greatly obscured: the smoke rose and spread in sheets among the branches of the trees. Most of our men fought kneeling as they fired, many of them behind trees, stones, and whatever cover they could get, but there were considerable groups that stood. Occasionally one of these groups, which had endured the storm of missiles for moments without perceptible reduction, would push forward, moved by a common despair, and wholly detach itself from the line. In a second every man of the group would be down. There had been no visible movement of the enemy, no audible change in the awful, even roar of the firing—yet all were down. Frequently the dim figure of an individual soldier would be seen to spring away from his comrades, advancing alone toward that fateful interspace, with leveled bayonet. He got no farther than the farthest of his predecessors.

Hazen attempted to hold on as long as possible and called on his commanders to send support. Several of his couriers were shot down before they could deliver his dispatches to the rear. With no help forthcoming, and the brigade receiving fire front, right and left, the Federals decided to retreat to safety. As Bierce remembered, the decision to fall back seemed to have been the common resolution of the troops rather than the commanders:

> No command to fall back was given, none could have been heard. Man by man, the survivors withdrew at will, sifting through the trees into the cover of ravines, among the wounded who could draw themselves back, among the skulkers whom nothing could drag forward.

The Rebel fire was so intense in places that some units were unable to extricate themselves and were pinned down in the Rebel front.

After Hazen's failure, Wood decided to renew the attack with Gibson's brigade around 1800. The Federals advanced over the ground that Hazen had covered and managed to get up against the Confederate line, only to suffer the same result as their predecessors. Trapped in a pocket of rifle and artillery fire, Gibson was likewise compelled to fall back.

After Gibson's failure, Howard and Wood were forced to admit defeat. However, Wood's last brigade, Knefler's, was sent forward to occupy Cleburne's troops so that the elements of Hazen's and Gibson's brigades trapped before the enemy line could fall back to safety, and the dead and wounded could be retrieved. Knefler's advance got underway around 1900 and managed to push within 100 yards of the enemy, where it held under the hostile frontal and flanking fire for most of the night.

The affair at Pickett's Mill proved to be another costly defeat for Sherman with the Federals losing 1,600 as casualties. Hazen's brigade lost some 500 men in the attack, while Gibson's command took 681 casualties. The Confederates suffered lighter losses of 85 killed and 357 wounded. Cleburne wrote in his report that the piles of dead Federals lying before Granbury's position were greater than many of his officers had ever seen before.

Elated by the Federal repulse at Picket's Mill, Johnston planned to launch a counterattack against the Federal left on the morning of 28 May. However, when Hood advanced against the enemy flank, he found the Federals well entrenched to receive the attack. Rather than copy the Federal defeat of the day before, Johnston canceled his aggressive move, and the Confederates retreated to the safety of their fortifications.

By 28 May, Sherman had decided to give up fighting around Dallas. Disappointed that he had not been able to win any successes against the Johnston's position there, the Federal commander decided to shift his forces to the northeast to get back on the Western & Atlantic Railroad. McPherson would be the first to move pulling out of his position near Dallas and moving behind the rest of the army to take up a position to the east, closer to the rail line.

Johnston quickly realized Sherman's intentions and planned to counter them. At first, Hardee was ordered to probe McPherson's lines with a reconnaissance in force. Hardee responded by setting Bate's Division move to the task. Bate's division advanced, letting out a yell which "the devil ought to copyright," in the words of one Federal, and the Confederates managed to engage some of Logan's corps in a short but fierce fight. At one point the Rebels won a small success when some troops captured guns of the *1st Ohio Battery* on Logan's right. However, the attack soon dissolved when Logan personally led a counterattack, shouting "give them hell boys," as his forces compelled the Confederates to retreat.

Despite Johnston's attempts to pin the Federals down, Sherman's army slowly extricated itself from the Hell-Hole at Dallas and inched its way east towards the Western & Atlantic. The legion of Federals slowly slogged its way through the rough terrain made worse by heavy rains, towards Acworth while, to the south, the Army of Tennessee shadowed its movements. On 1 June, Federal cavalry seized the previously formidable Allatoona Pass which had been left unguarded during the fighting around Dallas. By 6 June, Sherman's army was in Acworth and once again on its supply line. The Federals rested, rebuilt the railroad and once again received supplies. Meanwhile, Johnston was on his way south with his troops to take up a new position to block the next enemy advance.

CHAPTER VII

BEFORE THE THREE MOUNTAIN LINE

10 June - 18 June, 1864

*I*n planning the next stage of the campaign, Sherman was convinced of Johnston's unwillingness to remain above the Chattahoochee to contest the Federal advance. Presumably, the Rebel general was anxious to fall back to a position just north of Atlanta, where a decisive confrontation with the Confederates would take place. Sherman confided this belief to one of his subordinates on Monday 6 June, saying that he wanted to move his army to Marietta on Wednesday or Thursday and then proceed south to the Chattahoochee by Friday. The Federal commanding general would later find, to his intense irritation, that these expectations were somewhat unrealistic.

As Sherman's army rested from the trials endured in the soggy woodland of the Hell-Hole, 9,000 men of Major General Frank Blair's *XVII Corps* rejoined the *Army of the Tennessee* after enjoying a relaxing veteran furlough. These troops replaced the losses Sherman's army had suffered thus far in the campaign from combat, disease and the detailing of detachments to the rear. All in all, the combined strength of the armies of his command was still some 100,000 troops.

While Sherman's army recovered its strength at Acworth, Johnston was strengthening a long line of fortifications to the south. The Confederate line south of Acworth extended some 10 miles from Brush Mountain arcing out to the north at Pine Mountain before turning to the southwest for Lost Mountain. Hood guarded the Rebel left east of the Western & Atlantic Railroad where it curved around Brush Mountain. The center was under Polk with assistance from Bate's Division of Hardee's Corps which was placed in advance of the Confederate position on Pine Mountain. The right was defended by Hardee and William H. Jackson's dismounted cavalry at Lost Mountain. Though the Confederate chain of works at this three mountain line may have looked imposing with its parapets and numerous embrasures for well-protected cannon, it also contained defects which, if exploited, could seriously hamper any defense. The greatest weakness was at Pine Mountain. There, Bate's troops were positioned in a salient of the Confederate line, dangerously in the advance of the rest of the army and vulnerable to any powerful frontal and flank attack that Sherman might muster. Worse still, Johnston's current strength of 65,000 troops was tenuously stretched over the 10 miles of fortifications, across and along the three heights. As the Federals approached the line, the Confederate position appeared increasingly untenable.

On 10 June the Federal army advanced to test the Southern works. The *Army of the Tennessee* advanced on the right flank, down the Western & Atlantic Railroad. The *Army of the Cumberland* headed the main Federal thrust towards the Confederate center at Pine Mountain. Falling on Hardee in the area of Gilgal Church, between Pine and Lost mountains, was Schofield's *Army of the Ohio*. An almost constant heavy rain made the advance a long and tortuous affair. Sherman's troops negotiated crossings of flooded creeks and streams while thick mud trapped wagons, cannons, horses and even men. And all the while, Confederate pickets peppered away at the advancing Yankee columns. Still, the Federals managed to drive the Rebel skirmishers from their advance outposts and soon arrived in front of the main Confederate line.

At first, Sherman ordered his troops to close in on Johnston's works, but not to engage in any serious combat. Units of Thomas' *Army of the Cumberland* closed in on Johnston's weak point at Pine Mountain defended by Bate's Division. Palmer's corps

Lost Mountain at sunrise.

The crest of Pine Mountain after Bate's Division vacated the height. The Fighting Bishop, Leonidas Polk was killed on this spot by a Federal shell as he was taking cover from a Union bombardment.

was sent to the left, and Howard's to the right of the salient to threaten the Confederate position. By 13 May Major General Bate's troops faced the truly uncomfortable possibility of being attacked and cut off from the rest of the army.

The Federal movements caused Hardee increasing concern for the fate of Bate's Division. On the fourteenth, Johnston answered Hardee's request to inspect the division's emplacement and was joined in this endeavor by General Polk. While on

Leonidas Polk
1806-1864

Leonidas Polk was a North Carolinian by birth and a member of the West Point class of 1827. During his tenure at the Academy, he enjoyed a close friendship with Jefferson Davis and Albert Sidney Johnston. Shortly after his graduation, he resigned from the army to pursue a religious calling. In 1830, he was ordained in the Episcopal Church and quickly rose its hierarchy. By 1836 he was missionary bishop of the Southwest and after five years, was made bishop of Louisiana. When war broke out twenty years later, he took up the sword of the Confederacy.

Polk's close association with President Davis won him a command in the Upper Mississippi Valley. There he committed one of the greatest blunders of the war by seizing Columbus, Kentucky on 3 September 1861; an act that effectively drove the neutral Bluegrass State into allegiance with the Union and deprived the Confederacy of Kentucky's land, resources and population. Later, on 7 November, Polk managed to win a small victory at Belmont, Missouri against an obscure Federal officer by the name of Ulysses S. Grant.

After Albert S. Johnston assumed command of the western forces from the Appalachians to the Mississippi, Polk reverted to corps command and saw action in many of the major battles out West,

The Fighting Bishop, Leonidas Polk.

such as Shiloh, Perryville, Stone's River and Chickamauga. However, Polk's period of command with the Army of Tennessee involved him in a conflict of personalities with its commander, Braxton Bragg. Polk's contempt for Bragg was evident in his constant criticisms to President Davis and calls for the general's removal. Polk even resorted to open insubordination in some cases. After Chickamauga, the infuriated and fed up Bragg called for Polk to face a court martial for his misdeeds and refusal to obey orders during that battle. Instead, Davis protected his friend by shifting him to a new command in charge of the Department of Alabama, Mississippi and East Louisiana.

While in command of this department and the Army of Mississippi, Polk confronted William Tecumseh Sherman's raid against Meridian, Mississippi. Rather than offering any type of opposition, the bishop panicked and allowed Sherman to roam across Mississippi, wreaking destruction almost at will.

By May, Polk was returned to the Army of Tennessee as his Army of Mississippi was sent to reinforce Johnston against Sherman's assault on Atlanta. Throughout the campaign, Polk performed as a corps commander without special mention. At Pine Mountain on 14 June, the bishop's life came to a sudden end when he was struck and killed by an enemy shell.

A handsome and charismatic gentleman, Polk displayed no ability which could have earned him the positions of responsibility that he held throughout the war. His rank and commands stemmed more from his close friendship with President Davis than any demonstration of skill.

---

reconnaissance at Pine Mountain, Johnston, Hardee and Polk quickly recognized the apparent menace that the Federal movements posed to Bate's command. Johnston himself came to the conclusion that Pine Mountain had to be abandoned and the division withdrawn to safety.

As the Confederate officers inspected the enemy's position only 600 yards away with field glasses, the Yankees spotted them. The small group of Confederate generals and staff officers spying on his lines caused Sherman to exclaimed heatedly, "How saucy they are!" Irritated by their audacity, the Federal general then directed a battery to open fire on the group, to force them to seek cover. As most of the Confederate leaders scurried for safety under the opening bombardment, Polk nonchalantly

A Federal battery pounds the entrenchments of Major General William B. Bate's Division on Pine Mountain. Bate's advance position on Pine Mountain made his command vulnerable to a possible Federal attack on 13 and 14 May.

walked for the rear, apparently unconcerned about the oncoming barrage. Polk paid dearly for his imperturbable calm; he was cruelly mangled by a direct hit from an Federal shell. The deadly missive blasted through the unfortunate Bishop's chest, killing him instantly. Johnston expressed his sadness over the loss of a valued corps commander. "I would rather anything but this," he said, upon viewing the general's dead body. The vacancy for corps command opened up by Polk's demise was temporarily occupied by Major General William W. Loring, until he was replaced permanently by A. P. Stewart.

Polk's death did not long remain a secret from the Federals, who learned of the event from decoded Confederate signal messages. Sherman indifferently reported to Washington the next day, "We killed Bishop Polk yesterday, and have made good progress today." Just in case the Yankees were ignorant of the loss they had inflicted, Bate's Confederates left behind a note pinned to a tree on Pine Mountain as they abandoned the height. It read, "You damned Yankee sons of bitches have killed our old general Polk."

Over the next couple of days, the Federals engaged in several actions which made Johnston's lines untenable. On the fifteenth and sixteenth, the *Army of the Tennessee* and the *Army of the Ohio* were active on the Confederate flanks. Some success was scored on the left when McPherson's *Army of the Tennessee* managed to get Brigadier General William Harrow's division of the *XV Corps* around the Rebel right, capturing 320 soldiers of the 40th Alabama in the process. Farther off to the west, Schofield's troops got around the Rebel left, forcing the Confederates to retract their flank there.

Unable to hold the three-mountain line in the face of such threats, Johnston began to pull his army back. First he retreated to a new position on the high ground on the

Major General Joseph Hooker's Yankees of the XX Corps seize Lost Mountain in the wake of the Confederate retreat from the height.

Ranks of Brigadier Charles C. Walcutt's Brigade of Harrow's division of the XV Corps in action against the Confederate right at Brush Mountain on 15 June. Harrow's command managed to capture 320 Confederates during the confrontation.

Andersonville

Fewer names conjure up scenes of greater horror and misery in the annals of the Civil War than the Confederate prison Camp Sumter, located near Andersonville, Georgia. From February 1864 until September 1864, thousands of Federal prisoners, some captured on the fields of the Atlanta campaign, were crammed into its insufficient confines and struggled to survive without shelter, clothing, proper sanitation, water or food. Over the months of Andersonville's cruel existence, thousands of them died.

In 1863, the Confederacy was forced to consider a new site for a prison camp to hold captured Federals. The camp at Richmond, Virginia was increasingly unsatisfactory because of the city's close proximity to the enemy lines. There was always the danger that an enemy attack might liberate Federals located there creating incredible havoc. Further, there were scarcely enough supplies for civilians and troops in Virginia, and the needs of Federal prisoners only compounded the problem.

The site eventually picked for the new Confederate prison was located in Sumter County in southwestern Georgia near Andersonville, a small town on the South-Western Railroad, less than 100 miles south of Atlanta. The prison, which was named Camp Sumter, was intended to hold some 10,000 men. From the very beginning, Confederate authorities encountered difficulty after difficulty in attaining stores to build and supply the new camp. The site was far away from any source of supplies, and the local citizenry was not disposed to offer aide in any form as they were hardly enthusiastic about having a prison located so close to their homes.

While there was a great necessity for the new prison, irritating details blocked and slowed its construction.

Delays in getting permission to build the prison in the appointed area and lack of supplies forced the Confederates postpone work until January. Supplies and the labor of slaves eventually had to be impressed to start work on the project. Originally, the Confederates sought to build with wood planks because such materials would supposedly be cheaper than pine logs from a nearby forest. However, Southern mills were ill disposed to sell to the authorities at government set prices when the open market offered handsome profits. Thus, as prisoners began to arrive at Camp Sumter, nothing in the way of shelter had been prepared for them.

The first Federals arrived in February. The prison built to confine the incoming prisoners was only a crude stockade; a huge fence of 20 foot pine logs about twelve inches wide, set closely together in a five-foot trench. The perimeter was rectangular and enclosed around 16.5 acres with gates set up to the east and west for entry. On the outside were a number of elevated sentry posts, set up closely behind the stockade, about 80 feet from each other. These posts were roofed, accessible by a ladder, and built so that the bottom was three and a half feet from the top of the stockade. Fifteen feet from the interior of the stockade walls ran a post fence called the "dead line." Any soldier who strayed into the space between the fence and the stockade was warned to

View of the southwest stockade at the Andersonville prison camp.

retreat, or he would be shot. A small stream of water passed through and divided the camp, providing the water supply. No buildings were ever constructed, and the prisoners were left to their own devices to find shelter.

By February, Richmond was shipping 400 prisoners a day to be crowded into the stockade of Camp Sumter. From the very first, their stay was very unpleasant to say the least. The unfortunate Federals seemed to lack in almost everything. Shelter was constructed out of whatever they could possibly find, such as logs, tree limbs, bushes, blankets, tent flies and clothing. Sometimes this was supplemented by a hole dug in the red Georgia earth. These measures provided some shade from the sun, but did little to protect the soldiers when a heavy rain fell.

A bakehouse was supposed to be built to feed the incoming troops, but it was not finished until May of 1864. As a result, the prisoners' food was often unpalatable. Up to that time, the Confederates issued uncooked rations of meal, sweet potatoes and beef or bacon. Other

items such as beans, molasses, rice and vinegar couldn't be issued properly due to a lack of buckets. Some Federals were fortunate enough to receive bakepans, but most received no implements whatsoever with which to prepare or eat their food.

One terrible aspect of the prison was that no measures were ever taken to provide proper sanitation for the prisoners. The only facility was the creek running through the camp. The men were supposed to use the upper portion of the stream for drinking and the lower end for waste disposal. However, this was never enforced. A plan was created to build two dams within camp, one upstream to provide drinking water, the other further downstream to provide water for bathing. Floodgates were to be installed which when opened, would flush the collected filth out of the camp. However, the dams were never installed, due to a lack of supplies, and the sanitation problem was never clearly addressed.

Overseeing life at the camp and its deteriorating conditions was Captain Heinrich Hartmann Wirz. Wirz was a Swiss immigrant who had dabbled in tailoring and medicine before entering the war. He rose to the rank of captain and served the Confederate adjutant general. In December of 1862, he visited Paris and Berlin as a special ambassador for the Confederacy, but returned to the South in March 1864. He was then appointed to command Andersonville. Wirz has been variously represented as a brutal or a tragic figure. According to advocates of the North, Wirz subjected his prisoners to cruel punishment and continuous suffering, and even murdered some unfortunate Northerners. Sympathetic Southerners portray Wirz as the victim of

The execution of the commandant of Andersonville, Captain Heinrich Hartmann Wirz, on 10 November 1864. While Wirz was regarded as a war criminal in the North, some Southerners believed him to be a scapegoat and the United Daughters of the Confederacy even had a monument built in his memory.

an inadequate supply system which left him without the means to properly provide those in his charge.

Regardless of the debate over Wirz's supposed culpability, as more and more prisoners came to Andersonville, conditions in the camp continued to deteriorate. The problems were primarily the result of overcrowding. In March 1864, there were 7,500 prisoners incarcerated at Andersonville. By June, this figure had increased to 22,291 and a month later 31,678 prisoners were being held, three times the number that were originally intended to be incarcerated there. The prison was increased by ten acres to compensate for the massive numbers of arrivals, but this additional space still was not adequate enough to meet the needs of the inmates.

Food for the troops remained poor and scarce. The official ration dwindled to meager portions of meal, bacon or beef, with peas, rice, vinegar and molasses issued on occasion. Though Southerners point out that the prisoners received the same rations as the guards, the Federals' food was often poorly prepared. Once the bakehouse was finally finished it produced a bread that caused dysentery and bowel problems and even Wirz admitted that it was unfit to eat. Prisoner Captain J. H. Wright recalled of the bread rations that the Federals received:

> I know that the cook-house was very filthy; they used to knead up the dough in a trough, and it seemed to me as if it was shortened with flies; it was full of flies when they worked it up....You could break it open and see the flies in it.

Receiving inadequate nourishment from the Confederates, the Yankees were forced to find subsistence from other sources. Those Federals who were fortunate to retain money after their capture could purchase expensive goods from a sutler who was allowed to trade in camp. Some tried to get money or food by providing service as barbers or tailors, while others tried to win some funds through games of chance. A few industrious Federals built ovens to bake their own corn bread which was of better quality than that produced at the Confederate bakehouse. Still, many Federals became starved and emaciated and were driven to such extreme means as robbery and even murder to get food from their comrades. Some scoured the grounds for crumbs, even combed feces for food which had not been digested.

Unceremonious burial of Federal prisoners who died from the abominable conditions at Andersonville. Around 13,000 northerners died at the camp during its short existence.

Fresh water also remained a problem. The stream that was supposed to supply the troops quickly became an odorous cesspool of filth and excrement. Worse still, the stream served as a receptacle of much of the refuse discarded from bakery. One Federal told of the stream, "The most of the men had to depend upon the brook for their water, and that, at many times, was exceedingly filthy. I have seen it completely covered, almost, with floating grease, and dirt, and offal. I have gone in barefoot, when it was so dirty that I had to go out, as I was getting all over with grease and filth." Another remembered of swamp near the stream:

> The prison was very horrible on account of the filthy condition of it; the swamp which runs on each side of the small stream that runs through the stockade was so offensive, and the stench from it was so great, that I remember the first time I went down there I wondered that every man in the place did not die from the effects of the stench...it was a living mass of putrefication and filth; there were maggots there a foot deep or more....

Federal prisoners were forced to seek other sources of water. Some strong individuals dug deep in the earth near the stream to make wells. Fortunately, a heavy storm on 9 August alleviated the suffering in the prison. Not only did it wash away much of the filth, but it uncovered springs which provided the troops with a much better water supply. One such was called Providence Spring and described as a divine answer to soldiers' prayers for fresh water.

The state of the prisoners' clothes was close to abominable. Many of those who came from Richmond were already dressed in rags, and those who came directly from the battlefields wore uniforms dirty and threadbare from weeks and maybe months of campaigning. As the Confederacy could not even issue uniforms to its own men, there was no possibility that prison clothes would be issued to the captives. Usually the only option for new clothes was to steal from their comrades.

Worst of all, conditions were ripe for the spread of disease. Wastes, human and otherwise, were deposited all around the camp, without soap and water the Federals could not clean themselves. Not surprisingly lice, flies and other vermin multiplied. Diarrhea, dysentery and scurvy were rampant and went almost unchecked. Hospitals were set up for the sick, but none were admitted who could enter the facilities on their own strength. A few overworked surgeons attempted to deal with the hundreds of patients who came under their care. Lack of medical supplies as well as of adequate food and sanitation compounded the plight of the sick and denied recovery to many of them.

Andersonville was thus a veritable death trap. Over the months of its baneful existence, especially during the summer, the deathrate of captives soared. In July 1,187 prisoners died, in August there were 2,993 deaths, and for the following month the death rate declined to some 2,277. Of the 45,000 men who suffered the torture of Andersonville, 13,000 died from disease and the terrible conditions of life at the camp. Their bodies were disposed of ignominiously and without much ceremony. Both Federals and Confederates stripped a corpse of anything of value before the lifeless husk was carried to a shed called the "dead house" to await burial. Bodies were then deposited in six-foot trenches with a stake marking the name, regiment and grave number of the lost soldier.

Though the Confederates were culpable for the severe deficiencies in care, the Federal inmates compounded their own misery by victimizing their fellows. The gruesome overcrowding and the lack of guards to police the facility prompted robbery, violence and murder amongst the prisoners. In June, when only 1,500 guards were policing thousands of prisoners, a band of robbers and cutthroats called the Raiders were able to prey on their compatriots for several weeks. At first the group operated at night, but later they became more daring and stole and even murdered during the day. Other prisoners appealed to Wirz to take some action but he refused, claiming that he did not have the necessary authority. When the troops then asked for permission to organize a force to arrest and try members of the Raiders, the commandant gave his consent. A group called the Regulators rounded up 24 suspects, tried them, and convicted six who were considered the ringleaders. These men were sentenced to death and hanged by the Confederates on 11 July.

Andersonville's existence was threatened when Sherman took Atlanta and invaded the interior of Georgia. The specter of liberation forced the Confederates to dispatch troops to other camps in Georgia and South Carolina. Andersonville was actually liberated late in the war, after the Federals took nearby Columbus, Georgia on 17 April 1865.

After the war, the Federals looked to find a scapegoat for the conditions at Andersonville and the deaths that had occurred there. Captain Wirz appeared to be the best candidate. He was tried and found guilty of abusing and murdering prisoners after a multitude of bitter witnesses testified to his cruelty. As Wirz faced death on the gallows, he was supposedly offered a reprieve if he would implicate Jefferson Davis in the horrific treatment of Federal inmates at the prison. Wirz refused and was hanged on 10 November 1865.

During and after the conflict, both sides attempted to explain the catastrophe of Andersonville. Southerners claimed they lacked the resources necessary to sustain their own populace and armies, let alone Yankee prisoners. The problem was compounded by the depredations of the Northerners as they advanced into the Confederate heartland. Such advocates pointed out that the South did the best it could, while the North, with its greater wealth, failed to treat Rebel captives properly in such notorious prisons as Elmira, New York and Point Lookout, Maryland. Besides, the refusal of Northern generals to offer prisoner exchanges had caused the overcrowding of prisons in the first place. For their part, Northerners argued that the Southern refusal to treat captured Afro-American soldiers as prisoners of war led to the collapse of the exchange system. Moreover, Southern captives suffered a lower mortality rate than their Northern counterparts, and received better housing and food than Federals could hope for at places such as Andersonville. Either way, Andersonville was indicative of the ignorance, incompetence and cruelty of prison systems maintained by both sides during the war.

east bank of the Mud Creek, on the night of the sixteenth. Sherman was intensely eager to pursue and crush Johnston, but his attempts to pin down the Army of Tennessee collapsed due to command problems and heavy rain. By 18 June, Sherman's troops had finally gotten across the flooded Mud Creek with much difficulty and managed to get in close against the Confederate line, and pound a salient in the Southern position with a powerful infantry fire. At 2300 of that night, Johnston retreated two miles farther south to take up a stronger position, on Kennesaw Mountain.

The series of encounters before Johnston's three-mountain line included hardly any major battles, but, instead, was a week-long affair of extended, soggy skirmishes in the ever-present rain. Frustrated by his inability to force Johnston to engage in a pitched battle, or to get around his flank and into the Confederate rear, Sherman was coming closer to the decision to launch a full frontal attack to break the enemy's line.

Burial-ground for the some 13,000 Federal soldiers that died at Andersonville prison.

Sherman's army slogs its way through the muck and mire in pursuit of Johnston's army. The almost interminable rain of May and June trammeled Sherman's attempts to pin down Johnston's army north of the Chattahoochee

CHAPTER VIII

KENNESAW MOUNTAIN

19 June - 3 July, 1864

*K*ennesaw Mountain, one of the last great heights on the Western & Atlantic's path to Atlanta, offered Johnston one of his strongest positions during the entire campaign. The mountain was a large ridge broken up into three different sections which overlooked the roads to Atlanta and Marietta as well as the Western & Atlantic Railroad. The northernmost portion was the 700-foot Big Kennesaw, followed by a smaller height of 400 feet, known as Little Kennesaw, and a prominence at the end, known as Pigeon Hill. Most of these heights were heavily wooded, with a steep and treacherous ascent from the ravines at their base. The terrain made Kennesaw all but invulnerable to a direct attack once a strong force was entrenched there.

After Johnston's troops had slogged their way to the mountain through the muck and mire caused by the constant showers of May and June, they began to construct a strong set of entrenchments upon Kennesaw's heights. Loring's troops worked to fortify the crests of Big Kennesaw and Little Kennesaw, forming the Confederate center. Loring's old division and Major General E. C. Walthall's Division (previously Cantey's Division) took position on Big Kennesaw, while Little Kennesaw was occupied by French's Division. The Confederates managed to draw cannons up the heights, but only with considerable difficulty. While a road was found leading up to the top of Big Kennesaw, a trail had to be carved through the dense foliage on Little Kennesaw so that 100 men could bring up one piece of artillery at a time. After tremendous exertions, the Southerners managed to put nine guns on this height.

The rest of the Army of Tennessee was spread out to the north and south of Loring's position. Hardee occupied the left of the line with Cheatham's Division placed on a prominence soon to be known as Cheatham's Hill. Cleburne's, Bate's and Walker's divisions extended north to join Loring's corps. On the right was Hood's Corps, with his troops set up to protect the Western & Atlantic. Most of the Confederate soldiers found protection in the extensive network of lunettes, advance works, abatis and entanglements created in preparation for any Union attack.

Early on 19 June, the Federals discovered that the Confederates had retreated from their position at Mud Creek. Once again, Sherman was prematurely optimistic about the Confederate retreat and reported to Washington that Johnston was falling back to the Chattahoochee. Once again Sherman found that he had deluded himself when the Federals encountered stiff resistance as they fell upon the main Confederate line.

On the nineteenth, Thomas came up before Kennesaw and began to shell Confederate entrenchments on the heights. As the Federal batteries unlimbered to undertake their deadly work, the Southern soldiers on Kennesaw were at first confident that they were so high up on the mountain that the enemy artillery would not be able to hit them. As one Rebel remembered, they were soon proven wrong:

> The first shot from the battery in our front fell at the base of the mountain, and we cheered derisively. The next shot came halfway up the side, and the cheering was much fainter than before. The third shot struck the rocky cliff above our heads, and instead of cheers, there was anxious looking for spots that would afford some protection.

The fourth shot cut a couple of exposed Confederate soldiers in two. Learning their lesson, the Rebels remained under cover as the Federal artillery blasted away at the heights with devastating precision.

At first Sherman hoped to flank the southern extension of the Confederate line. As McPherson moved in to occupy Loring's men, and Thomas took positions before Hardee, Hooker's *XX Corps* and Schofield's *Army of the Ohio* attempted to sidle around the Confederate flank to the south.

As Hooker and Schofield moved against the Confederate left, Johnston grew increasingly concerned at the threat which the Federals were posing to his flank. The commander of the Army of Tennessee chose to block the move by bringing Hood from the right to take position in front of the National forces then struggling to move around the Confederate left. Hood's troops marched out on the night of the twenty-first to trudge south, while some of Loring's men and dismounted cavalry occupied their vacated trenches. After passing through Marietta, Hood's command arrived before Hooker's and Schofield's positions early on the 22 June and began to entrench.

As the Federals of the *XX Corps* and *Army of the Ohio* attempted to advance in the direction of Marietta on 22 June, they captured Butternut troops claiming to belong to Hood's Corps. This information fueled expectations of a coming battle and the Federals struggled to entrench in an area near the Powder Springs Road and the farm of a Peter Kolb. Hooker took the left, Schofield was on the right and heavy artillery was brought up to strengthen the line.

At 1700, Hood answered their suspicions by launching an impetuous attack against the opposing Federals. His folly soon became evident, for Hood's men were faced with charging over open ground, or advancing through thick underbrush which broke and intermingled the strict formations necessary to attack well entrenched positions. The Rebels fell victim to blasts of case shot and canister fired from 40 cannons massed to meet the attack. Though the heavy fire played havoc with the Confederate ranks, some Rebels managed to advance to within 35 yards of the Federal line before the attack finally collapsed. One Federal wrote of Hood's failed attack:

> We could see their officers rush before the men with waving sabres, striving to rally them, but in vain; for our artillery and musketry were showering lead like hailstones

Entrenchments During the Atlanta Campaign

Amongst the many contributions to modern warfare devised during the Civil War was the common use of extensive entrenchments. While entrenchment had been a military practice since the dawn of organized warfare, it gained a particular importance during the War Between the States. Due to the longer range and increased accuracy of the rifle over the dated musket, the stand and fight infantry tactics of the Napoleonic line of battle became obsolete. The devastating toll of the rifle, especially on attacking soldiers, forced troops to seek various forms of cover rather than by remaining out in the open to suffer death or injury. Well-defended entrenched positions were often invulnerable to the most powerful attacks, as Sherman found during the battles of Picket's Mill and Kennesaw Mountain. Later in the war, offensive and defensive forces alike were and engaging in a form of trench warfare. In the Atlanta campaign, both Confederates and Federals almost instinctively dug in during many of their confrontations. In his memoirs, Sherman described this peculiar kind of warfare:

> The enemy and ourselves used the same form of trench, varied according to the nature of the ground, viz.: the trees and bushes were cut away for a hundred yards or more in front, serving as an abatis or entanglement; the parapets varied from four to six feet high, the dirt taken from a ditch outside and from a covered way inside, and this parapet was surmounted by "a head-log," composed of the trunk of a tree from twelve to twenty inches at the butt, lying along the interior crest of the parapet and resting in notches cut in other trunks which extended back, forming an inclined plane, in case the head-log should be knocked inward by a cannon-shot. The men of both armies became extremely skillful in the construction of these works, because each man realized their value and importance to himself so that it required no orders for their construction.

The instinct to entrench became so embedded in the Federal character that Sherman's soldiers automatically picked positions to fortify without the direction of engineers or the help of sappers. However, Sherman began to employ freed slaves to build his fieldworks, allowing his troops to rest. Bondsmen were used in a similar manner by Johnston.

By the end of the war, entrenchments were the rule rather than the exception on most Civil War battlefields. This type of activity was later utilized during the bloody campaigns of World War I.

Part of the extensive network of fortifications around Atlanta. Before trenches are palisades and chevaux-de-frise. Atlanta's fortifications were so impressive that Sherman was forced to place the city under a time consuming siege while he cut its railroads rather than attempting to take it by a direct attack.

90 / THE ATLANTA CAMPAIGN

Advancing troops of Hood's Corps are cut down by Yankees of Schofield's and Hooker's commands at the battle of Kolb's farm on 22 June. Hood lost some 1,000 men in an ill-advised and fruitless assault while inflicting only a small number of casualties on the Federal commands that opposed him.

into their lines. After repeated assaults, the panic-stricken rebels, with broken ranks, riderless horses, and trailing banners fell back to their works.

After the charge disintegrated, Hood's men fled for cover; 1,000 men had fallen as casualties. The Federals lost only some 350 men.

The battle itself was not as important as a dispute that arose in the Federal leadership over the actions of General Hooker. During the battle, Sherman queried Hooker about the peril of his situation. The general responded that his command was holding its own but was facing three corps of the Army of Tennessee, and he was unsure about the safety of his extreme right flank, protected by Schofield at the time. While Sherman found it difficult to believe that all three corps of the Army of Tennessee were threatening Hooker, he was concerned that Schofield might have failed to follow instructions to protect Hooker's flank. When Sherman rode to the

right the next day, he learned to his irritation that Hooker had called for help when one of the divisions of the *XX Corps* hadn't even been engaged. Sherman met with the commanders of the *XX Corps* and the *Army of the Ohio* to discuss the events of the previous day. Schofield was incensed by Hooker's dispatch, believing that "Fighting Joe" was impugning his battle leadership, and bitterly requested Sherman to go to the front to see whose dead lay farthest in the front, to prove which command had been more actively engaged. Sherman then berated Hooker for giving a sensational report and for insinuating Schofield's incompetence. Sherman would later write, "I reproved him more gently than the occasion demanded, and from that time he began to sulk." Hooker's resentment over the episode, and his perceived ill-treatment by Sherman, would lead to another confrontation with his commander later in the campaign.

By mid-June of 1864, Sherman was growing increasingly annoyed by his failure to deal a serious blow to Johnston's army. In his bitterness, he began to lash out against many of his subordinates. His petulant criticism encompassed attacks against the cavalry and its leaders, who were described in the general's dispatches to Washington as fainthearted and almost useless. However, Sherman's most biting condemnation fell on Thomas and the *Army of the Cumberland*. Sherman belittled Thomas for maintaining an extensive wagon train for his headquarters while the rest of the army was stripped down to the bare essentials for speed. The general wrote of Thomas' troops, "A fresh furrow in a plowed field will stop the whole column, and all begin to intrench." As the frustrated Sherman marshalled his army towards the strong Confederate line at Kennesaw, he had in mind a direct assault on a position that would be almost invulnerable to such an attack.

Originally, Sherman had not planned to attack Johnston at Kennesaw. On 5 June he wrote Halleck, "I expect the enemy to fight us at Kennesaw Mountain, near Marietta, but I will not run head on against his fortifications." Through early June, Sherman continued to tell Halleck that he would turn Johnston at Kennesaw rather than confront him there. By 21 June Sherman had changed his mind. He wrote Halleck on that day, "The enemy still holds Kennesaw....I am ready to attack the moment the weather and roads will permit troops and artillery to move with anything like life."

Despite the imposing nature of Johnston's Kennesaw position, Sherman believed the time and place was advantageous for a major attack. First, he believed the aggressive change in strategy from flanking to a direct attack, would catch Johnston by surprise. Second, Sherman was under the impression that Johnston's troops were stretched thin across the six-mile front that they occupied at Kennesaw. Hopefully then, the Federals could make a quick strike against the unsuspecting Rebels, break through the painfully thin Confederate lines and get into the enemy rear. Sherman had reason to expect victory, as a similar attack had been successfully launched at Missionary Ridge during the battles around Chattanooga in November, 1863.

On 24 June, Sherman issued his orders for an assault against Kennesaw Mountain, detailing an attack to get under way three days later, at 0800. Thomas was to launch the major thrust with part of his army while making the necessary demonstrations to assist its success. McPherson would support Thomas' assault by launching a diversionary attack and engaging the Confederates in his front. Schofield was to keep active, threatening the Confederate left. If Johnston's army cracked under these

View of Kennesaw Mountain from a Federal signal station on Pine Mountain.

Federal entrenchments at Kennesaw Mountain. Despite the impressive array of Confederate works on and nearby Kennesaw, Sherman launched an attack against Johnston there on 27 June and suffered his most costly repulse during the entire campaign.

combined movements, Thomas might be able to get into the Confederate rear and seize the Western & Atlantic Railroad south of Kennesaw.

Both Thomas and McPherson picked the ground where their troops would make their assaults. Thomas opted to hit a salient in Hardee's line at a hill held by Cheatham, with an attack by Jefferson C. Davis' division of the *XIV Corps* and Brigadier General John Newton's division of the *IV Corps*. McPherson decided to strike further off to the north between the southern extension of Little Kennesaw and Pigeon Hill. As these Federal troops moved into their positions, a constant and fierce fire from artillery and pickets was maintained by both sides. Since his arrival before Kennesaw, Sherman had massed several hundred cannons to pound the Confederates on their mountain stronghold. The ferocity of the shelling led soldiers to exclaim that Sherman meant to take Kennesaw or fill it full of iron.

As dawn rose on the fateful day of the twenty-seventh, many Federals were clearly daunted by the tasks that lay ahead of them; some even had premonitions of death. A colonel in Colonel Daniel McCook's brigade of Davis' division, Oscar F. Harmon, penned his wife a farewell letter, knowing well that he might not survive the coming fight. When correspondent Dennis Conyngham wished luck to Brigadier General Charles G. Harker, a brigade commander in Newton's division, and expressed his hope that the officer would return safely, Harker responded, "Well, I hope so, a soldier should always be prepared for death though....They are powerful works; we can never take them; I will do my best though." Colonel McCook, a former law partner of General Sherman, tried to inspire his men by reading lines of the stirring poem, "Horatius at the Bridge":

94 / THE ATLANTA CAMPAIGN

Confederates engage in the incredibly arduous task of hauling guns up the face of Little Kennesaw. Some one hundred men were needed to pull just one artillery piece up the mountain.

Colonel Daniel McCook. McCook was mortally wounded leading his troops during the doomed Federal attack at Kennesaw Mountain.

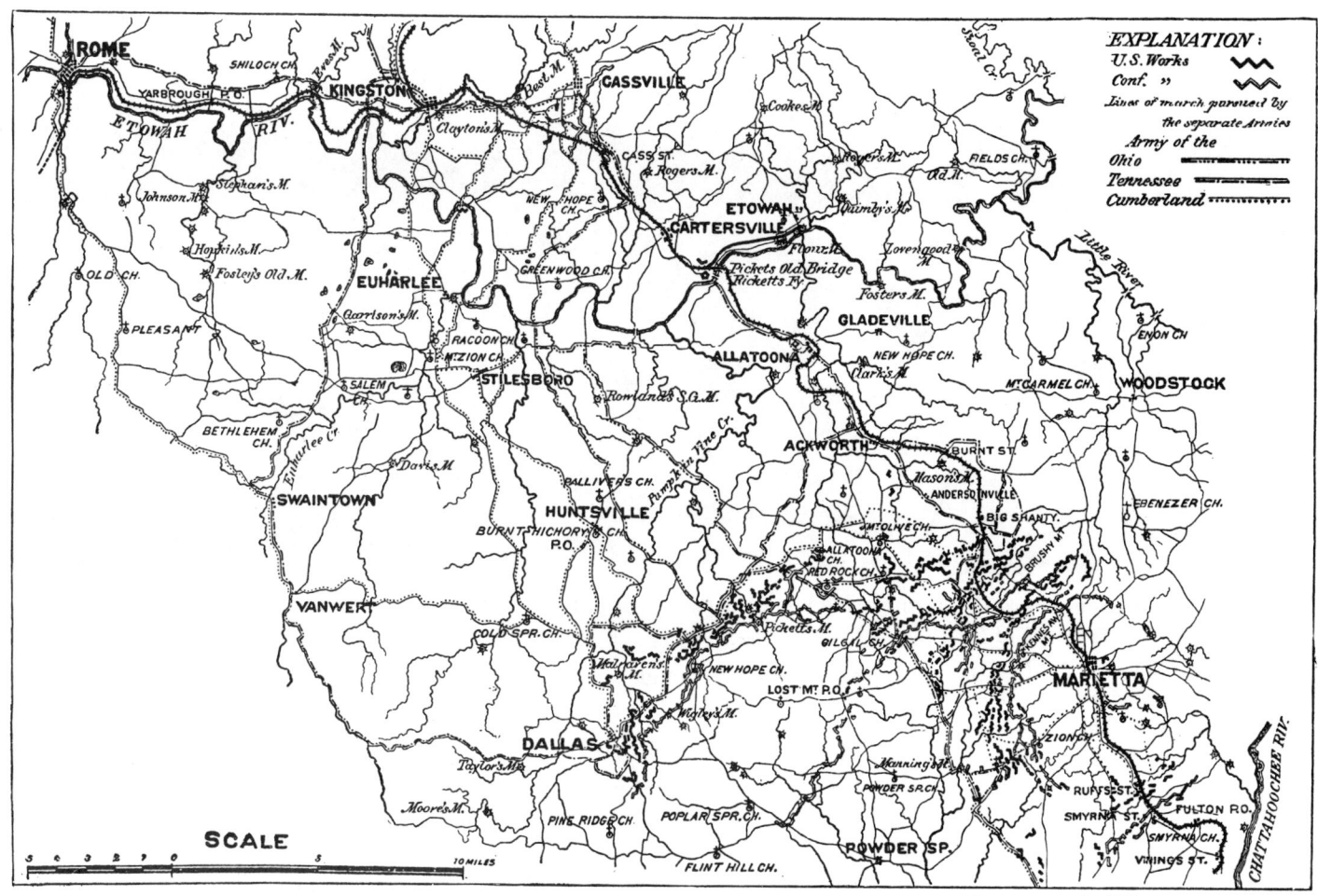

Action around Kennesaw Mountain.

And how can men die better
Than facing fearful odds

For the ashes of his fathers
And the temples of his Gods.

As morning passed, picket fire and barrages from Federal artillery swelled in a terrifying crescendo. By 0800, the Federals of the *Army of the Tennessee* were swarming towards the Confederate line. The 5,500 men of Morgan L. Smith's division of Logan's *XV Corps*, supported by Brigadier General Charles C. Walcutt's brigade of the same corps, took the offensive driving for the gorge between Little Kennesaw and Pigeon Hill that was held by French's Division of Confederates. The Federals engaged in a ferocious struggle with tenacious Southern pickets amongst the trees and boulders covering the path towards the Rebel line. Throughout the advance, Smith's men

A fierce battle rages on Kennesaw Mountain during the attack of Logan's XV Corps on the position of Polk's Corps commanded by Major General W. W. Loring.

Brigade commander in Brigadier General Charles G. Harker. During the battle of Kennesaw Mountain, Harker led his troops mounted on a white charger. A conspicuous target, he was shot down and killed during the fighting.

contended with a thick forest of trees, boulders, bushes and vines. In some places, the Federals were forced to crawl forward through the "natural abatis" to move forward or slog their way through a knee deep swamp. The whole line quickly lost its formation as it struggled to advance through the tangled terrain, but continued on. Once up against the main line, the Federals were finally brought to a halt by entanglements and heavy gunfire. "Officers and men fell thick and fast," remembered Smith. Confederate Major General French reported that "so severe and continuous was the cannonading that the volleys of musketry could scarcely be heard at all on the line." Unable to make any headway, the Federals retreated with heavy casualties. Some 850 men were killed and wounded in the unsuccessful assault. Stricken by the huge losses, General Logan is said to have wept over the fateful slaughter of his troops before Kennesaw.

While McPherson's attack sputtered and failed, Thomas' main attack got under way to the south. Newton's and Davis' divisions and their supports got under way an hour late, around 0900. Brigades of both units were grouped into columns of regiments to maintain the momentum of the attack and deliver a sledgehammer-like blow against the Confederate line.

Thomas' massed infantry quickly fell victim to a tremendous fire as it crashed through the woods to attack the line held by Cleburne and Cheatham. One Confederate, Thomas A. Head, recorded of the Federal advance:

> As they came up through an open field their ranks closed up into a solid phalanx, and appeared as so many living walls of blue. Their arms glistened in the sunlight, and the columns advanced as steadily as though they were on dress parade.

As the Federals advanced, they suffered from withering fusillades. One Yankee later recalled that "the air seemed filled with bullets, giving one the sensation experienced when moving swiftly against a heavy wind and sleet storm."

Davis' division advanced, with McCook's brigade on the left and Colonel John G. Mitchell's on the right, against Cheatham's hill. McCook managed to get within a few feet of the Confederate line, but no farther. A couple of flag bearers fought their way forward to plant their standards on the Rebel works and some valiant souls leaped up on the entrenchments to grapple with the Butternuts in hand to hand fighting, but no real inroads could be made. Colonel McCook himself managed to climb the Rebel works, waving his sabre as he urged his troops on shouting "Forward the flag!" When one of his soldiers asked the colonel to take cover, McCook yelled back, "God damn you, attend to your own business." McCook paid dearly for his gallantry, falling mortally wounded. As he was taken from the field, he managed to call out to his men, "Stick to them boys." McCook's successor, Colonel Harmon soon fell with a minie ball through his heart. Colonel Caleb J. Dillworth then assumed command, but the remnants of the brigade were only able to dig in and hold a position several yards in front of the Confederate ranks.

Mitchell's brigade on McCook's left suffered the unfortunate fate of being caught in flank by Confederate artillery and was literally blown away. Despite the terrible musketry and artillery fire, these troops still managed to get close enough to the Southern trenches to engage in hand-to-hand combat before they were forced to surrender, retreat or take cover.

To Davis' left, Newton's division advanced with Harker on his right, and Brigadier General Nathan Kimball and Brigadier General Wagner's brigades on the left. These Federals suffered the same terrible fate as Davis' men before the Confederate entrenchments. Harker's brigade managed to remove the obstructions which had been laid in its path and get in close to the Confederate line with its commander riding amongst his troops on a white charger, a most conspicuous target. Harker ignored the fire until he and his steed were shot down. Harker's men pressed forward, and a color bearer got close enough to the Confederate line to place his standard on the Rebel

Troops of the Army of the Cumberland *attack Confederate entrenchments south of Kennesaw Mountain. Though Thomas' troops managed to reach the Confederate fortifications at numerous points, they were unable to break through and were shot down in great numbers.*

Deed of Honor at Kennesaw Mountain

After Newton's division bloodied itself on the Confederate entrenchments at Kennesaw Mountain, the unit retreated for safety, leaving a great number of casualties behind. These unfortunates soon became endangered by a blaze set alight by the discharges of musketry and artillery. Colonel William H. Martin of the consolidated 1st and 15th Arkansas saw the threat to the enemy wounded and called for his troops to cease fire. He then tied a handkerchief to a ramrod and climbed the Confederate works to call out to the Federals, "We won't fire a gun till you get them away. Be quick." The Federals returned to recover their wounded with the help of Martin and some of his men. A Federal major gave Martin a set of fine pistols in honor saying, "Accept them with my appreciation of the nobility of this deed."

View of Kennesaw Mountain from Little Kennesaw.

works only to be stabbed to death by Rebel bayonets. Soon the Federals had no recourse but to seek cover. Newton's two other brigades under Kimball and Wagner, also engaged the enemy, but they too, were repulsed with heavy casualties by the deadly Confederate artillery and musketry.

Thomas' casualties throughout the day were horrendous: Davis lost 824 men in his attack, while Newton suffered 654 casualties. One Federal wrote of the failed attack, "We were mown down like grass." Another reported that his Yankee comrades "fell like ripened wheat before the reaper."

After the Federal attacks were smashed against the Confederate entrenchments, Sherman was informed of the failure of his assault and that heavy casualties had been suffered. Originally, Sherman had intended to continue pounding away at the Army of Tennessee until victory was won but Thomas dissuaded him, saying "We have already lost heavily today without gaining any material advantage. One or two more such assaults would use up this army." Sherman gave up the attempt to break through Kennesaw, his efforts having cost him 3,000 casualties in contrast to his Johnston's relatively meager loss of around 700 men.

While the rest of the army bloodied itself at Kennesaw, Schofield's *Army of the Ohio* was off to the west winning a real success by turning Johnston's flank. On the twenty-seventh, Schofield got across the Olleys Creek and gained access to the Sandtown Road, which led to Johnston's rear. Sherman called this movement the "only advantage of the day" and planned to make good use of the opening.

Over the next few days, the opposing armies squared off against each other from trenches on the Kennesaw Mountain line and engaged in both warlike and pacifist endeavors while Sherman plotted. The character of the fighting was such that in some places it was impossible to raise a hand or head above field works without drawing a shower of bullets. At other points, troops on both sides called informal truces to trade Federal coffee for Confederate tobacco. On 30 June, a general truce was called to bury the rotting dead left unceremoniously exposed on the field of battle for three days.

Troops of McCook's brigade were entrenched only 30 yards from the Southern line and engaged in an ingenious pursuit during their post-battle stay at Kennesaw. Taking advantage of their close proximity to the Confederates, they began digging a tunnel under the Rebel works. The plan was to plant explosives in the mine under their adversaries on 4 July to celebrate the National birthday. However, the rude prank was never set off for the Federals and Confederates were on the move again by early July.

Sherman decided to use Schofield's gains of 27 June to flank the Confederate left by pulling McPherson out of line to the north of Thomas, in order to link up with Schofield's right. The move would not only threaten Johnston's Kennesaw position, but would post the Federals five miles from the Western & Atlantic Railroad and only three miles from the last natural barrier to Atlanta, the Chattahoochee River. On the evening of 2 July, McPherson moved out. To mask the noise of an army in motion, blankets were bound over the wheels of caissons and cannons.

However, the Confederates were also on the move. Johnston had come to realize that the Federals would soon be closer to Atlanta than he was. On 2 July, he decided to fall back to Marietta. By the morning of 3 July, the Federals who remained before Kennesaw found the enemy had vacated their trenches.

Sherman had received a cruel education in the futility of direct attacks on entrenched positions by his rash assault at Kennesaw. After that debacle, he returned to his tried and true strategy of flanking the enemy. Still, the Kennesaw episode had not been a total failure. Johnston had been forced to relinquish his strong position and fall back to the rolling terrain around Atlanta which would be harder to defend. Better still, the heavy rains of May and June had finally ended, allowing roads and fields to dry. Now Sherman's army would be able to actively engage Johnston in a war of maneuver in which the Federals' greater numbers would provide a enormous advantage. Johnston, on the other hand, was drawing closer to Atlanta than many in the Confederacy would have liked. If he was to protect his position at the head of the Army of Tennessee, he would have to act quickly and decisively.

The National colors fly over Marietta, Georgia. On 3 July, the streets of the town were teeming with Federal troops as Sherman pressed his army to catch the Army of Tennessee as it retreated south from Kennesaw.

CHAPTER IX

TO THE CHATTAHOOCHEE

3 July - 18 July, 1864

With Kennesaw abandoned by the Confederates, Sherman actively attempted to engage his adversary in a major battle before he could cross the Chattahoochee. Johnston reacted with a series of gradual retreats that avoided a confrontation on Sherman's terms, but allowed the Yankee armies to get closer and closer to Atlanta, a city of critical importance to the Confederacy. Though Johnston claimed to have a plan to best the Yankees before they could seriously threaten Atlanta, his actions displayed little desire for any aggressive initiative, but only an ambition to delay and retreat.

After taking Kennesaw, Sherman pursued Johnston south through Marietta until he found the Confederates occupying a strong set of earthworks outside of Smyrna Station. The entrenchments were six miles in length, from Rottenwood Creek on the north to Nickajack Creek in the south and had been prepared before Johnston's arrival by engineers and slave labor. Sherman believed that the earthworks were merely one last desperate attempt by Johnston to hold off the Federals while he attempted to cross the Chattahoochee. As he told Thomas, "Johnston's halt is to save time to cross his material and men. No such a general as he would invite battle with the Chattahoochee behind him."

Sherman seemingly ignored the lessons of Kennesaw and planned for Howard's corps to attack the Confederate line on 4 July. Despite success in taking advance rifle pits, Howard's offensive ground to a halt before the main line of entrenchments. When Howard described the tremendous obstacle he faced, Sherman downplayed his fears: "Nonsense, Howard, he is just laughing at you." Howard solemnly replied, "You will see, General." At 1000, Howard's forces moved forward across a cornfield, toward the Rebel works and almost certain death. The Confederates were no doubt morbidly exultant at the chance to massacre the advancing Federals and held their fire in order to deliver a massive volley at close range for the deadliest effect. When the

Yankee Generals view Atlanta from a signal station on the northern side of the Chattahoochee. At the far right holding the field glass is Major General John A. Logan of the XV Corps. To his left is Major General Joseph Hooker, commander of the XX Corps and sitting at center is Brigadier General Peter J. Osterhaus, a divisional commander in Logan's corps.

Federals closed to within 200 yards of the Southern line, Sherman wisely called off the ill-conceived attack and Howard's Federals halted to dig in. The Confederates, indignant at the lost chance to slaughter the enemy, immediately opened an angry fire on them.

While Howard's men avoided disaster, a more successful attack was launched on Independence Day. Brigadier General John W. Fuller's brigade from Major General Grenville M. Dodge's corps of the *Army of the Tennessee* was directed to attack the Confederate works near Ruff's Mill. While the Federals prepared to launch the assault, Colonel E. F. Noyes reminded his troops of the *39th Ohio* that they could ill afford to be defeated on this of all days; it would be improper to have the home papers report that the regiment had been ignominiously defeated by Rebel forces on the birthday of the Republic. Recognizing their responsibilities, Fuller's men charged, only to run into an abatis some 100 yards in front of the Confederate line. Coolly breaking through the obstruction, Fuller's men took a moment to reform and then pressed forward once again and took the Southern works. Noyes himself fell with a wound to the ankle. While he was being carried to the rear to receive attention, he called out to Generals McPherson and Dodge: "I got their works and they got part of mine; but its Fourth of July, and I don't care a continental." The Federals suffered 140 casualties for their victory.

However, an even greater Federal success was attained on the right, where Major General Frank Blair's corps managed to get around the Confederate left under Hood. Hood then complained to Johnston that the left was in growing danger and would not hold for long under a major attack. Finding his position near Smyrna Station now untenable, Johnston decided to fall back three miles to the south for a new defensive line.

Johnston's new emplacement was a masterwork of defensive fortifications, designed by his chief of artillery, Brigadier General Francis A. Shoup, and prepared while the Confederate army was still at Kennesaw Mountain. Unlike the trenches and breastworks usually employed on Civil War battlefields, Shoup's fortifications were a series of mutually supporting triangular redoubts, twelve feet thick and twelve feet high. The line of these forts bent back in a six-mile crescent guarding the railroad crossing over the Chattahoochee, with each flank resting solidly on the river. Shoup designed his fortifications so that they could be held with a small number of troops while the rest of the army struck at the flank of any Federal force trying to cross the Chattahoochee, either north or south of the Confederate position.

Sherman had no intention of attacking such imposing Confederate fortifications. Instead, he sought to nullify Johnston's position by finding another viable crossing over Chattahoochee. Besides the three covered by Johnston's defensive works, there were many more places to cross to the east and west, but most of these had been rendered unusable by the heavy rains of late spring and early summer which had swollen the river. However, Sherman decided to try his luck in flanking Johnston to the east. Though this move was less direct than an attempt to cross downstream, it would allow the Federals to protect the railroad in their rear, and also to threaten the Georgia Railroad which connected Atlanta with the East and Richmond. McPherson was sent south to demonstrate against the Confederates while Thomas occupied the Confederate front. Meanwhile, Schofield and Garrard's cavalry division were sent upstream to seek out an appropriate crossing.

On 8 July, Schofield located an suitable point where the Soap Creek joins the Chattahoochee. Schofield had men of Colonel Daniel Cameron's brigade of Cox' division cross the river on a submerged fish dam to brush off a detachment of Rebels on the opposite bank, while the *12th Kentucky (USA)* crossed in pontoons downstream. By 1530, Cameron's brigade was under way. The current was strong and a few men slipped and fell, but they were helped up by their comrades, and all crossed safely. The *12th Kentucky (USA)* managed to get across without much difficulty, under a covering fire from Colonel Robert K. Byrd's brigade of Cox's division. The Confederate force of militia and cavalry supposed to block the enemy's crossing wasn't in much of a mood to contest the Federal movements and only fired a few shots before fleeing. Once the Federals were on the other side, and sure that the bank was clear, more troops were ferried across in pontoon boats while engineers set about building a bridge. By nightfall, the structure had been completed, and a division was across on the south bank of the Chattahoochee, threatening Johnston's rear, Atlanta and the Georgia Railroad.

Garrard's cavalry also effected a crossing, albeit in a somewhat comical fashion. Some of his troops waded through the muddy waters under fire from Confederate troops on the opposite bank. Since the Federals were armed with Spencer repeating carbines and their ammunition consisted of metallic cartridges, they could reload their guns under water. Thus, the Yankees advanced sunk down in the river, rose up when ready to fire, and sank back into the water to reload. The bizarre spectacle stunned Confederates; some of them even ran down to the bank of the Chattahoochee to surrender, just to get a look at the guns that could be loaded under water.

Johnston, who had expected and prepared for an attempt to cross south of his position, was taken completely by surprise by Sherman's crossing upstream. With the Federals already over the river, Johnston decided to retreat to find a better position to contest the Federal advance. He hoped that this would be provided by the outer works of Atlanta, south of Peachtree Creek.

Richmond was increasingly irritated by Johnston's Fabian strategy and his apparent failure to avert Sherman's movement on Atlanta. The ranks of officials and politicians calling for Johnston's dismissal were growing and becoming ever more difficult to ignore. President Davis himself was under intense pressure from Georgia politicians who believed that Johnston was going to lose the Peach State without even fighting a major battle. Cabinet members, including such old supporters of Johnston as Secretary of War Seddon, also advised that the general be relieved. Though Davis himself was displeased with Johnston's behavior, he faced the dilemma of finding the replacement for the general once he was relieved. The president found himself in the same quandary as several months earlier, in November of 1863: who could be appointed to lead the Army of Tennessee and win a major victory?

For the moment, Davis tolerated Johnston's retreats, but as the general fell back to and across the Chattahoochee, the president increasingly pestered him for some impression of his plan to block Sherman. Davis first sent his military advisor and former commander of the Army of Tennessee, Braxton Bragg, to investigate Johnston's situation and possible strategy. Bragg arrived on 13 July and his first report was hardly inspiring. The Federals were threatening to fall upon the Georgia Railroad, thus cutting off Richmond from most of Georgia, Alabama and Mississippi. At the same time, Johnston seemed more prepared to abandon the city of Atlanta than to fight in its defense. Supplies and machinery were being readied for transportation elsewhere, while most of the population was leaving the city. Davis came to the opinion that Johnston must either demonstrate that he would fight for the Atlanta or be replaced by somebody who would.

On 16 July, Davis demanded to know Johnston's future plans. Johnston's reply, on the same day, was not to the president's liking for the general seemed to be ready to give up Atlanta to the Federals. First, Johnston reported in his curt dispatch to Davis, "As the enemy has double our number, we must be on the defensive. My plan of operations must, therefore, depend upon that of the enemy. It is mainly to watch for

Members of Major General Grenville M. Dodge's XVI Corps *of the Army of the Tennessee ford the Chattahoochee near Roswell's Ferry on 9 July.*

Confederate Neutrality During the Atlanta Campaign

With Sherman and his Yankees engaged in a ruthless campaign of destruction to exhaust the enemy's capacity to wage war, Confederate businessmen were forced to pursue various schemes to save their assets. One of the more ingenious ruses was employed at Roswell, Georgia, a small town just north of the Chattahoochee.

On 4 July, Federal cavalry under Brigadier General Kenner Garrard, entered the town which contained a textile mill employing a large number of female workers. Curiously enough, the French tricolor was flying from the factory. The reason for the flag's unexpected presence so far from France, was found when the mill's owners approached Garrard. Claiming to be French citizens, they demanded that the Federals protect their property as neutrals in the conflict.

At first the confused Garrard bought the ruse, but the next day he took the opportunity to inspect the mill closely. Despite the claims of supposed neutrality, the initials "C.S.A." were being woven onto the bolts of cotton. Enraged by the attempted deception, Garrard sent the workforce home, closed the factory and later burnt down the mill. With Sherman's permission, Garrard then rounded up the factory's female employees and had them shipped to Marietta, from where they were deported to Indiana. While Union generals claimed that this act was for the protection of the workers, the incident sparked a myriad of Confederate myths about separated families and searches by the citizens of Roswell to find their lost relatives and spouses after the war.

Another attempt to feign allegiance to a foreign nation took place near Atlanta shortly after the fall of city. Colonel Oscar L. Jackson's regiment was preparing to burn a large amount of cotton when a Southern civilian approached him. He warned the officer that the cotton belonged to the Belgian consul, and that the Federals would incur deep trouble for disturbing the property of a citizen from a neutral country. Jackson later wrote in his diary, "I told him that was bad for the Belgian consul...as I proposed burning it anyhow. I burnt what in the market would be worth $30,000. An hour did the work."

Though considerable ingenuity and audacity was exercised, there is little evidence that these ruses actually duped the destructive Yankees.

---

an opportunity to fight to advantage." This had been Johnston's strategy throughout the entire campaign, and had so far resulted in Sherman being able to move into the interior of Georgia and threaten Atlanta. Further, Johnston stated that he was planning to leave the defense of the city to the Georgia Militia troops for a day or two so that the Army of Tennessee could enjoy greater mobility. This action seemed unlikely to guarantee the safety of a city so vital to the Confederacy as Atlanta. To Davis, all indications were that Johnston had failed him and the Confederacy.

The president came to the conclusion that Johnston would have to be removed. His search for a suitable replacement centered on Hood and Hardee. For advice about Johnston's removal, Davis turned to his foremost military confidant, Robert E. Lee, suggesting that Hood might be appointed to command of the Army of Tennessee. Lee replied that it would not be advisable to remove Johnston at such a critical stage in the campaign. However, if the general had to be relieved, Lee doubted Hood's ability to succeed in the position; he suggested Hardee should fill the post. Davis' military advisor, Bragg, was reluctant to support such a move. Bragg maintained an intense dislike for Hardee and vigorously argued that his former subordinate lacked the competence and initiative to solve the present crisis. Instead of gambling on Hardee, Bragg supported Hood who seemed like a tough fighter, such as the Army of Tennessee desperately needed at this black hour. Davis' decision was to be just as

Tired of the war, Confederate soldiers surrender to Yankee pickets.

controversial as his appointment of Johnston, back in December of 1863; he decided to replace Johnston with John Bell Hood. In the process, Hood was to be promoted over Hardee to full general. Command of Hood's corps was given temporarily to B. F. Cheatham until the arrival of the unit's new commander, Lieutenant General Stephen D. Lee. On 17 July, Johnston received word that he was being relieved of command in a letter from Adjutant and Inspector General Samuel Cooper which read,

> I am directed by the Secretary of War to inform you that as you have failed to arrest the advance of the enemy to the vicinity of Atlanta, far in the interior of Georgia, and express no confidence that you can defeat or repel him, you are hearby relieved from the command of the Army and Department of Tennessee, which you will immediately turn over to General Hood.

Davis' decision was welcomed in some quarters of the Army of Tennessee, but many men felt that the move would prove detrimental. One Rebel wrote of Johnston's relief,

> There was great indignation among the rank and file and there were open threats of insubordination....We had unlimited faith in the generalship of "Old Joe," as we liked to call him. We were willing to fight at any time and any place he said so believing that he would not ask us to fight, unless the advantages were clearly on our side. Of General Hood we knew little—only the impression prevailed that he was rash to a criminal extent.

John B. Hood
1831-1893

One of the great Confederate warriors of the Civil War was Kentuckian John B. Hood. Hood graduated a somewhat undistinguished forty-fourth in the West Point class of 1853. Between his graduation and the Civil War, he served in the infantry and cavalry, on garrison duty and frontier posts. After the guns of Sumter sounded, First Lieutenant Hood resigned from the National Army and headed south to take a similar rank in the Confederate forces.

Hood rose through the ranks quickly, attaining the rank of brigadier general, and went on to command a brigade of hard fighting Texans at Gaine's Mill, Second Bull Run and Antietam. In October, Hood received further reward in the form of a major generalcy and divisional command in Longstreet's Corps.

During the second day of Gettysburg, 2 July, the Kentuckian narrowly missed superlative success when his troops came close to turning the Federal left. Unfortunately for Hood, the possibilities of the moment were lost. The general fell with a wound which crippled his left arm, and his division was repulsed.

Following his recovery from the Gettysburg injury, Hood took to the field again when Longstreet was transferred west to join the Army of Tennessee. There, Hood's division managed to participate in the breakthrough of the Federal line at Chickamauga on 20 September 1863. During the battle, Hood suffered more ill luck when fell wounded again, this time with an injury that would require the amputation of his right leg.

Though Hood was a shattered image of a man by 1864, struck down by horrible wounds while he was still fairly young, his capacity for hard fighting was recognized with a promotion to lieutenant general and a corps command in the Army of Tennessee. Throughout the At-

General John B. Hood

lanta campaign in late spring and early summer of 1864, Hood performed competently although he secretly criticized Johnston's defensive postures and reluctance to attack. When Davis decided to replace Johnston, he chose the virtual antithesis of that general, the hard fighting Hood, to protect Atlanta from Sherman's depredations.

Possibly Hood was not fit for such a command. His wounds constantly bothered him and he had to be strapped onto his horse in order to ride. However, Davis believed Hood's fiery temperament was unyielding and appointed the Kentuckian to the rank of full general, giving him the reigns of the Army of Tennessee. Hood remained true to his character and engaged in a series of costly attacks against Sherman's Federals. The end result was defeat which forced Hood to abandon Atlanta.

Undaunted, Hood continued to take the offensive and drove into Tennessee in the hope of forcing Sherman to follow him. All that resulted was a pyrrhic victory at Franklin, Tennessee and a devastating defeat at the hands of George Thomas at Nashville in the winter of 1864. The Army of Tennessee was almost destroyed under Hood's leadership.

After his massive failures in Tennessee, Hood asked to be relieved, a request which was granted by Davis. Hood saw no service for the rest of the war. After the conclusion of the hostilities, he settled in New Orleans, married and had a huge family of eleven children. He also wrote his memoirs which defended his failures, criticized his subordinates and blamed the loss of Atlanta on Johnston. Unfortunately, however, the fortunes of the Hood family were decimated by a yellow fever epidemic. It destroyed Hood's wealth and killed him as well as his wife and several of their children.

Hood was an aggressive fighter, known more for launching forceful blows than putting much thought behind such attacks. Like so many generals who suffered serious failures, he was mistakenly advanced to commands beyond his natural ability.

108 / THE ATLANTA CAMPAIGN

Confederate fortifications on the Marietta Road, north of Atlanta, Georgia.

Howard's IV Corps crossing the Chattahoochee River to assail Atlanta.

When the Federal commanders heard of the change, they correctly expected that Johnston's passive tactics would be replaced by fierce attacks. Sherman learned from Schofield, an old classmate of Hood's at West Point, that the Confederate leader was bold to the point of rashness. Sherman therefore notified all of his subordinates of the change of enemy commanders, and of the probability of future Confederate attacks. Two days later, Hood would oblige the Federals with an offensive at Peachtree Creek.

The seventeenth of July marked the turning point of Confederate strategy during the Atlanta campaign. Hood was a direct contrast to Johnston; while the latter refused to risk taking chances, Hood had been schooled by Lee's daring gambits out East, which had won major victories despite overwhelming odds. It remained to be seen if Hood was the man to adopt such strategies and tactics successfully against Federal opponents in the West.

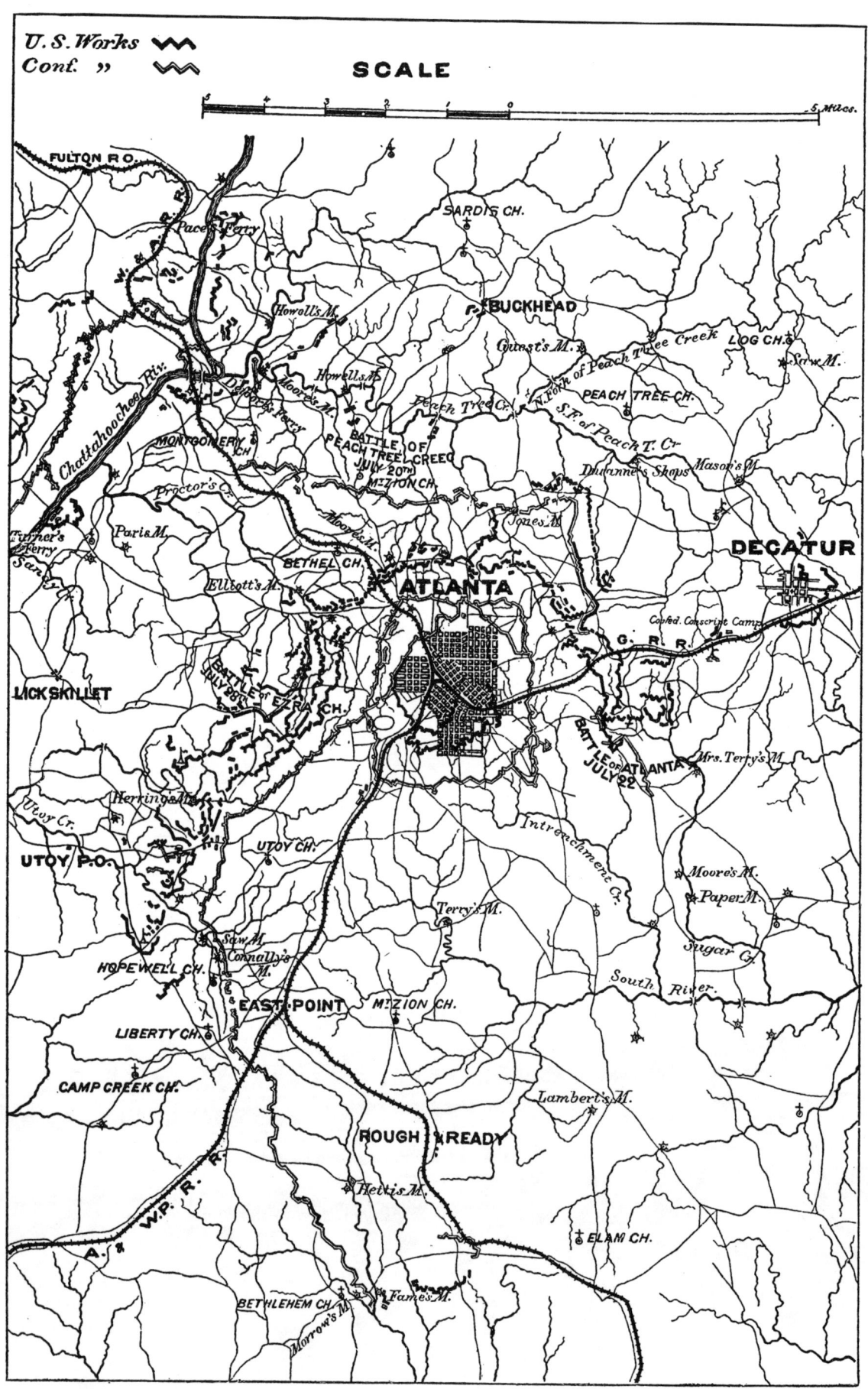

CHAPTER X

PEACHTREE CREEK

18 July - 20 July, 1864

Three months had passed since the beginning his advance, and Sherman's armies had now marched 120, miles to the gates of the city of Atlanta. The importance of the city to the Confederacy meant that the Army of Tennessee could retreat no further and would finally have to engage the Yankees in a decisive confrontation. Confederate Secretary of War Seddon related to the new commander of the army, General John Bell Hood, the immense responsibilities that weighed on the general's shoulders as he took command of the Army of Tennessee; "You are charged with a great trust. You will, I know, test to the utmost your capacities to discharge it. Be wary no less than bold....God be with you."

The immense significance of Atlanta also made the seizure and or destruction of the town of special import to Sherman. Succeeding in this task would accomplish his directive from Grant, calling for serious damage to the Confederacy's war resources. However, to take Atlanta, Sherman had to destroy its railroads: four lines radiating out of the city to various vital points of the Confederacy. Sherman was already in possession of the Western & Atlantic, which left the Georgia Railroad heading into Atlanta from the east, and the Atlanta & West Point and Macon & West Point railroads which connected the city with southern Georgia and Alabama. With all these lines cut, the Army of Tennessee would be forced to abandon the city, and the Confederacy would thus lose the productive, commercial and transportational resources of Atlanta and the surrounding area. The Federal armies would have to be wary as they maneuvered before and around the city to accomplish such tasks for the Army of Tennessee's new commander would look for the opportunity to hit, and hit hard.

Once across the Chattahoochee, Sherman's first task outside of Atlanta was move his army south of the Peachtree Creek and destroy the Georgia Railroad. This act would cut off the Army of Tennessee from Richmond and kill any chance of Robert E. Lee moving south to join Hood and threaten the Federals before Atlanta. In moving upon the railroad, Sherman had Thomas advance on Atlanta from the north to hold the Confederates in their entrenchments; Schofield headed to Decatur to

George H. Thomas
1816-1870

Probably one of the most competent generals and army commanders on either side, and truly the most unrecognized, was a Virginian who remained loyal to the Union, the imperturbable George H. Thomas.

Thomas proved his ability at West Point, where he graduated twelfth in the class of 1840. His service after West Point included fights against the Seminoles, frontier and garrison duty, and distinguished action in the Mexican War which won him two brevets. An injury Thomas sustained during his career made riding a horse painful. Unable to have his steed break into a gallop, Thomas was given the nickname of "Old Slow-Trot."

Thomas was recovering from an arrow wound sustained during his service on the frontier when the Civil War broke out. While many of his compatriots from Virginia flocked to the standard of their native state, Thomas chose to remain with the Union. His ability would prove to be an immense boon to the North over the coming years.

A brigadier general by the summer of 1861, Thomas achieved one of the first great National victories of the war by crushing a Confederate force under Felix Zollicofer at Mill Springs in Kentucky, on 19-20 January 1862. The stocky Virginian was promoted to major general four months later and saw service as a corps commander in many of the great battles of the West, including Perryville, Stone's River and Chickamauga. Before Perryville, Lincoln was prepared to promote Thomas as replacement for the conservative Major General Don Carlos

Major General George H. Thomas

Buell at the head of the army confronting Braxton Bragg in Kentucky. However, Thomas refused to assume command from his superior at such a critical moment. Later, at Stone's River, Thomas counseled his commander, Major General William Starke Rosecrans, to remain on the field and strengthened the general's resolve to wring a victory out of a nearly disastrous battle on 31-2 December 1862. However, it was at Chickamauga where Thomas won his greatest fame. After the Confederates had broken through the line of the *Army of the Cumberland* near Chickamauga Creek on 20 September 1863, Thomas remained on the field and maintained a stalwart defence in the face of overwhelming odds. His holding action allowed the *Army of the Cumberland* to retreat to safety at Chattanooga and won him the nickname of "the Rock of Chickamauga."

This near disaster led to the relief of Rosecrans and his replacement by Thomas at the helm of the *Army of the Cumberland*. His later efforts at Missionary Ridge and during the Atlanta campaign, especially at the battle of Peachtree Creek on 20 July, assisted in transforming the Federal war effort in the West into an unstoppable tide towards victory. Instead of participating in the March to the Sea, Thomas was detached by Sherman to deal with John B. Hood's Army of Tennessee, which was heading north into Tennessee. Thomas met the army at the battle of Nashville on 15-16 December 1864 and nearly annihilated the force.

After the war, Thomas continued in military service, and by the time of his death was the commanding general of the West Coast. While Thomas' services to the Union have long gone unrecognized in most historical accounts of the war, probably the greatest affront to his memory was contrived by his own family. His sisters, who were staunchly loyal to the Confederacy, refused to mention the name of their brother after he had joined sides with the hated Yankees. The bitter siblings even went as far as to turn his portrait towards the wall so as to manifest their hatred for Thomas and his many deeds which led to the downfall of the Confederacy.

The cost of battle. Crude graves mark the resting places of Federal soldiers killed at the battle of Peach Tree Creek on 20 July, 1864. Beyond the graves are entrenchments that the Yankees held with èlan during the course of the battle.

destroy the Georgia Railroad there, and McPherson fell upon the line and moved east along its tracks, tearing them up as he went. The Federals were under way on 17 July.

Hood had only been in command for a few days when he noticed a perfect opportunity to launch a crippling blow against the threatening Yankees by striking at the *Army of the Cumberland*. On 18-19 May, the troops of the *Army of the Cumberland* reached and began crossing the Peachtree Creek, to their peril. The movement left the force incautiously separated from the rest of Sherman's command by a two-mile gap. With the left of the *Army of the Cumberland* exposed, Hood could strike the force on its defenseless flank while it was involved in the act of crossing the stream. In doing so, Thomas' entire army might be seriously crippled, or very possibly destroyed. At a night meeting with his subordinates on 19 July, Hood conspired to have Hardee and A. P. Stewart hit Thomas the next day at 1300 and drive the *Army of the Cumberland* back west, against the Chattahoochee River. The Confederate plan involved an *en echelon* attack initiated by Hardee's Corps hitting the Federal right, with Bate's Division attacking first, followed on the left by Walker's and Maney's. Stewart's command, of Loring, Walthall and French, would then come in on Hardee's left to continue the attack up the Federal line. Cleburne's Division was to be kept in reserve, to exploit any weaknesses in the Federal line. Cheatham's men, supported by Wheeler's Cavalry and 5,000 troops of the Georgia Militia, would prevent the rest of the Federal army from coming to Thomas' aid. Hood himself would not witness the battle with his troops. Instead, he chose to remain four miles away from the action in Atlanta, leaving Hardee to oversee the advance.

The unsuspecting *Army of the Cumberland* was still on the move in the early morning of the twentieth. Thomas was engaged in crossing the Peachtree Creek while Schofield and McPherson were closing on Atlanta, the latter following the Georgia Railroad from the east. The troops of the *Army of the Tennessee* soon came to within two and a half miles east of Atlanta, close enough to bombard the city with artillery.

Atlanta During the War

Atlanta was swept up by secession fever in 1861 like many other cities in the South. Citizens joyously celebrated South Carolina's departure from the Federal Union and later the secession of the Peach State on 19 January 1861. Proud of the ebullience and promise of their city, Atlantans lobbied to have the town made the seat of Confederate government, but lost out to Montgomery, Alabama and later Richmond, Virginia.

As citizens throughout the North and South took up arms, hundreds of young men from Atlanta departed for the fields of destiny in Virginia, Kentucky, Tennessee and Mississippi. Meanwhile, Atlanta was turned into an arsenal for the Confederacy. Gunsmiths were brought to the town for the purpose of creating armories, while the machine shops of the Western & Atlantic Railroad were converted into forges to make weapons. The importance of this productive capacity increased substantially when the Confederacy lost the wealth of middle Tennessee, in early 1862. As the war progressed, Atlanta's factories were producing vital supplies of small arms, cannon, tents, canteens, belt buckles, buttons, shoes and other items of clothing. Warehouses around the town were loaded with goods needed by the armies in the field. Atlanta's importance as a transport hub was also demonstrated, as thousands of troops and tons of supplies passed through on trains to support the Confederate forces in action.

Early in the war, Atlanta appeared to be blissfully removed from the ravages of the conflict, but this impression quickly began dissipated as signs of war began to appear in the city. In May of 1862, the commander of the Army of Tennessee, Braxton Bragg, placed the city under martial law; the right of habeas corpus was suspended, the military patrolled the streets and blacks were forbidden to move around at night. The horror of war was displayed to Atlantans when their town became a major convalescent center for thousands of Confederate wounded. Many buildings, including the Atlanta Female College used to house the maimed until they healed.

As the conflict continued, Atlanta began to suffer the strains caused by the displacement of thousands of civilians. Throughout the war years, its town's population swelled with soldiers, refugees and the wounded. By 1863, the population had risen to 20,000 and by 1864 it housed some 22,000 people. This huge increase resulted in a series of civic difficulties. Prices rose, crime became prevalent and outbreaks of disease occurred periodically. A housing shortage forced refugees to make use of any form of lodging available, such as empty train cars and tents.

In 1863, as the future of the Confederacy seemed uncertain, Southern authorities began to see the necessity for entrenchments around Atlanta. Lemuel Grant, the chief engineer of the Department of Georgia, conceived of a plan to completely surround the city with ten miles of fortifications. Trees were cleared from 1000 yards before the town to provide a glacis for an unobstructed field of fire, and the wood was employed for gun platforms and revetments. Slaves were put to work on making the entrenchments, which were completed by December of 1863. The line was strengthened by 77 heavy guns and by April of 1864 this arsenal of ordnance included two siege guns. Throughout the winter of 1863-1864, the defenses of Atlanta were continually strengthened because an attempted Federal assault into Georgia seemed likely.

Over the late spring and summer months of 1864, the citizens of Atlanta waited in apprehension as General Joseph E. Johnston continued to yield ground to the Federal army under Major General William T. Sherman. When Johnston was replaced by Hood, just as the Federals were crossing the Chattahoochee to fall on Atlanta, the town's citizens were relieved and hoped that some hard fighting would send Sherman retreating back north.

On 20 July, the Federals began a light bombardment of the town. The opening shot came at 1300, from Captain Frances DeGress' 20-pound parrotts of *Battery H* of the *First Illinois Artillery*. The first casualty was a little girl, killed by an exploding shell. As the Federals swarmed around Atlanta, Sherman ordered a

A bombproof constructed by some of the citizens of Atlanta to help them weather the fierce Federal bombardment of the city.

The city of Atlanta, Georgia.

round to be fired into the town every 15 minutes to notify its citizens that National forces were threatening their city. The Federal hordes and the bombardment persuaded many civilians to leave the town. Those who stayed dug bombproofs and avoided buildings and landmarks that presented likely targets for enemy fire.

On 9 August, Sherman set about making Atlanta "too hot to be endured." A massive bombardment was maintained for about a month and 5,000 shells were thrown into the city by Federal cannon. Fires broke out, buildings were destroyed, and civilian casualties were incurred. During the bombardment, a family of six was killed when their bombproof was struck by a direct hit, one woman was struck down and killed while ironing her clothes, and a little girl was cut in two by a shell that came through the roof of her house. Despite the heavy shelling of the town, only some 20 civilians were killed. Many Atlantans were able to boast about surviving close calls, such as the 30 women shopping at a market when it was blasted by Federal shells. Though somewhat shaken by the experience, the women were otherwise unhurt. Hood protested the bombardment as uncivilized but Sherman disagreed. Considering the town a military target, he continued shelling the town.

All of a sudden the bombing stopped on 25 August. The next day it appeared as though the Federals had abandoned their works for they were nowhere to be seen. The battered but exhilarated citizens celebrated what they thought was Sherman's retreat. Bands took to the streets playing stirring music as townspeople thanked the soldiers who had been their protectors, and some offered prayers of thanks in church. Over the next few days, the Atlantans were to learn the awful truth; Sherman had not retreated, but had only maneuvered around the Atlanta to sever the town's last remaining railroads.

By 1 September Hood was preparing to abandon Atlanta to the Federals. The citizens were gripped by terror and many seized any means to escape the burnt out city. Since Atlanta's railroads were effectively destroyed, the Confederate commissary officers opened the doors to the warehouses and allowed civilians take whatever they could carry. After the Confederate troops had departed, all the stores which had been left behind including an ammunition train were fired. A massive inferno of immense destructive power ensued. One resident recalled of the explosions which shook Atlanta that night,

> The very earth trembled as if in the throes of a mighty earthquake. The houses rocked like cradles, and on every hand was heard the shattering of window glass and the fall of plastering and loose bricks.

The next day, the mayor of the city officially surrendered the town of Atlanta. Federal troops then began to occupy the city, a once thriving center of commerce which was now no more than a burnt out husk.

A battery armed with twenty pound parrott rifles soon opened up throwing shot and shell into the streets and houses of the once idyllic town. Their first victim was a little girl, killed by an exploding shell while on a walk with her parents.

At 1300, the *Army of the Cumberland* was still in a vulnerable position as its troops continued the process of crossing the Peachtree Creek. However, irritating difficulties prevented the Confederates from launching an attack at the prescribed hour and taking advantage of the situation. The trouble began when Hood was forced to reorganize his lines due to the rapidity of McPherson's advance. To block McPherson's troops moving on Atlanta, Hood ordered Cheatham to relocate his corps south, to fully cover the Georgia Railroad around 1000. Hardee's and Stewart's Corps were then to close up on Cheatham's Corps to shorten the resulting gap. When Cheatham moved, he accidentally went two miles farther than Hood had intended, throwing the rest of the army into confusion. The effect was chaos in the Confederate lines; the rest of the army moved around 1300 and spent over an hour finding new positions.

By the time Hood's attack got under way, Thomas' troops were across the Peachtree Creek, entrenched and in an advantageous position to receive an attack. Newton's division of Howard's corps was on the left, guarding the flank, while Butterfield's division of Hooker's command (under William T. Ward because Butterfield had fallen ill) was on the right, slightly recessed from the rest of the corps. The rest of Hooker's position had Geary on the left and Williams on the right. An inviting gap existed between the divisions which could pose a threat to the Federals if the Rebels found a way to exploit it. Palmer's corps occupied the right, but would hardly see any action on the twentieth. The ground in front of the Federals was rough and rolling, interspersed with streams, bogs, trees and shrubs. Any attack against Thomas' army would be extremely difficult, and success uncertain.

The bad luck which had plagued the Southerners all day continued when they opened their attack, as one of Stewart's divisions, under Loring prematurely attacked before Hardee. At 1400, Hardee had reported to Stewart that all was ready for the coming attack. Thus informed, when Loring saw Maney's Division advance into a wood on his right, he mistakenly presumed Hardee that was on the move and pressed his troops to attack at 1445. What he had actually seen was only Maney's troops maneuvering to readjust their lines.

Before Loring ran into the main Federal line, elements of his division engaged the *33d New Jersey*, which had been readying an advanced position for a battery. The Federals bravely stood their ground against the oncoming Butternut ranks in order to buy time for the rest of Thomas' army to prepare for the coming attack. Despite a tenacious stand, the regiment was thrown into a panicky retreat when the overwhelming numbers of Loring's division swarmed around their flanks. The unit lost six commissioned officers, half of its men killed, wounded and captured, and its regimental colors during the fateful encounter.

Loring then slammed into Ward's and Geary's divisions of Hooker's corps. Geary described the attack in his report of the battle:

> Pouring out from the woods they advanced in immense brown and gray masses (not lines), with flags and banners, many of them new and beautiful, while their general and staff officers were in plain view, with drawn sabers flashing in the light, galloping here and there as they urged their troops on to the charge. The rebel troops also seemed to rush forward with more than customary nerve and heartiness in the attack.

A victorious "Fighting Joe" Hooker rides his lines after his troops repulsed a Confederate attack at Peachtree Creek on 20 July 1864. Despite Hooker's hand in the victory at Peachtree Creek, he asked to be relieved from command soon after the battle due to a dispute with Sherman.

Loring's right brigade, under Brigadier General Winfield S. Featherston, managed early gains but was pushed back by a Yankee counterattack. Loring's left brigade under Brigadier Thomas M. Scott, came under a telling fire from Federal artillery and musketry from Ward's and Geary's divisions. Some Confederates attempted to lie down and bear the fire; others tried to flee, but ran into officers with drawn swords who were to hold the lines steady. Finally, unable to stand the vollies of National musketry, Loring's troops fell back.

Hardee eventually got under way about a half an hour after Loring had started the Confederate attack. Bate's Division advanced against the Federal left, but veered off to the northeast, away from the combat, to wander around in a wood. Some of Bate's men managed to find their way to the Federal flank, but were easily repulsed by Newton's reserve brigade belonging to Brigadier General Luther P. Bradley. Walker's division attained some success, taking part of Newton's works, but fell under an enfilade and was forced to fall back. Maney enjoyed the greatest fortune of all of Hardee's divisions by getting on Newton's right defended by Brigadier General Nathan Kimball's brigade. Under severe pressure, Kimball refused his threatened flank to save his brigade, and thus withstood Maney's attack.

The rest of Stewart's Corps, which got under way around 1600, enjoyed about the same measure of success as his compatriots on 20 July. Major General Edward C. Walthall's Division advanced on Stewart's right. His right brigade under Colonel Edward O'Neal managed to exploit the gap between Geary's and Williams divisions and subjected the Federals to a devastating fire which threatened to break their line. So intense was the Confederate musketry that many of the spokes on the wheels of Lieutenant Henry Bundy's Pennsylvania battery, on Geary's right, were split in two by minie balls. However, Bundy was able to wheel his guns to face the oncoming Southerners, while Geary refused the flank and blasted the Southerners into a retreat.

Walthall's left brigade, under Brigadier General Daniel H. Reynolds, managed to get onto the Federal works belonging to Williams, but was likewise forced to retreat.

By 1800, the gunfire had slowed from a deafening roar to the intermittent pop of picket fire. Hood's first fight had led to the loss of 2,500 of his own men, while inflicting a substantial loss of 1,750 men on Thomas's *Army of the Cumberland.*

The battle of Peachtree Creek was a most disappointing Confederate defeat. The assault of the Confederate divisions had been completely bungled. Most of the attacks failed to support each other and were thus doomed to fail. Worse still, Confederate numbers had not been fully utilized, for French's Division, much of Bate's Division and all of Cleburne's Division had missed the combat completely. The Confederate assaults completely failed to budge Thomas, let alone drive him into the Peachtree Creek and the Chattahoochee, as Hood had intended. The Federal troops, on the other hand, were delighted with the results of the battle. One remarked that it was the first time that the Confederates had fought on fair terms and it had turned out to be a total disaster.

CHAPTER XI

THE BATTLE OF ATLANTA

21 July - 22 July 1864

Though Hood's first offensive at Peachtree Creek had proven to be a major failure, the hard-fighting Confederate was not yet interested in adopting the defensive postures of Johnston. Instead, Hood remained true to his reputation and sought another opening to deal Sherman a decisive and destructive blow. Shortly after the conflict on the twentieth, Hood saw such an opportunity, this time against McPherson's *Army of the Tennessee*, then driving towards Atlanta from the east along the Georgia Railroad.

On 21 July, McPherson's troops engaged the Confederates in a short sharp fight for a prominence south of the Georgia Railroad east of Atlanta, known as Bald Hill. As McPherson approached Atlanta, he found that Bald Hill dominated the path of the Federal advance and the city of Atlanta itself, making it of vital importance to both Federal and Confederate armies. At the time of McPherson's advance the Confederates maintained a tenuous hold on the hill. Troopers from Wheeler's cavalry had dug in there on 20 July and, before dawn of the next day, Cleburne's Division arrived at the position to relieve the cavalry and strengthen the Southern grip on the prominence. By 0700, McPherson's *Army of the Tennessee* arrived before the hill and set to work bombarding the opposing Confederates with heavy artillery. Despite the cover of entrenchments, the Rebels suffered heavy casualties from the raining shells. Some 140 men were wounded or killed in the space of a few minutes. One well-placed missile alone decapitated six men and wounded twelve others.

McPherson intended to take Bald Hill by having Brigadier General Mortimer D. Legget's *Third Division* of Blair's *XVII Corps* attack the Confederate forces there, with support on their right from the *Fourth Division* under Giles A. Smith. Legget's division duly advanced against the hill and overwhelmed the Confederates. On the right, Smith ran into trouble on his advance under heavy fire from Cleburne's Confederates, causing the right of Legget's command to suffer due to lack of support.

Part of the extensive series of fortifications built around Atlanta to protect the city from enemy attack.

Men of the *20th Illinois* on the extreme right of Legget's line took such a fierce enfilading fire that the unit was forced to lie down. Anyone who attempted to rise or stand fell lifeless or wounded, his body riddled by minie balls. An Iowa regiment and a battery of howitzers were sent to refuse the right of Legget's *Third Division* and protect the Federal flank from collapse. Upon arrival, the combined might of these units blasted away into silence the irritating Rebels who threatened the right. While little headway could be made against the Confederates in Smith's front, Legget's Yankees had captured an ideal position from which to threaten Atlanta with artillery pieces as well as to command the surrounding area. Cleburne sought to retrieve Confederate fortunes by driving the Yankees back from Bald Hill, but the powerful attacks of his crack division proved insufficient to accomplish the difficult task.

The Federals had lost 728 men in their battle for Bald Hill, which was thereafter renamed Legget's Hill. Before the battle, Colonel George F. Bryant of the *12th Wisconsin*, a regiment that had seen very little combat thus far in the war, appealed to General Legget, "Now, general, if you have any fighting to do, give us a chance." Legget assured him that his men would get an opportunity. Indeed they did, for the regiment was hotly engaged in the fight for Bald Hill and lost 29 men killed and 108 wounded. After the battle, Colonel Bryant told Legget, "Your prophecy was too true and fulfilled much sooner than any of us expected." Cleburne lost only 300 men but recorded that the fight was one of the "bitterest of his life."

The seizure of Bald Hill caused Hood a great deal of consternation and forced him to confront the threat posed by the *Army of the Tennessee*. Besides the fact that a vital prominence overlooking Atlanta had been seized, Hood was concerned that the Federals might attempt to sweep around the Confederate army and strike at the Macon & Western Railroad. However, fortune was with the Confederate general. Wheeler's cavalry reported to him that the left flank of the *Army of the Tennessee* was exposed and dangerously vulnerable. Hood decided to take advantage of this opportunity by launching a major assault against McPherson's left in a manner reminiscent of some of Lee's campaigns, such as Chancellorsville. First, the Army of Tennessee was to be pulled back from its advance entrenchments to the main lines before Atlanta. From there, Hardee's troops would march in an arcing movement to the southeast, and then turn northeast to get on McPherson's left flank and rear by dawn of the twenty-second. As Hardee's Corps engaged in its surprise attack, Cheatham's Corps was charged with hitting the Federal army's front while Stewart held off Thomas to the north.

On the night of the twenty-first, all was under way. After midnight, Hardee's Corps tardily trekked through the city south and then turned to the northeast towards Decatur. On the march, the deteriorating condition of the Confederate army became increasingly apparent to soldiers, officers and civilians. While moving through Atlanta, some Rebels left the ranks to rob and loot stores, an act which did little to inspire the confidence of the populace. The 15-mile-long march took its toll on soldiers already weary from the fighting of the twentieth and the twenty-first. Exhausted men struggled through the unbearable heat of the Georgia night, gagging on the choking dust kicked up by tramping feet. Hundreds of troops fell by the wayside to seek rest when they were unable to go any further. One Confederate recalled of the appearance his comrades as dawn rose on 22 July, "When morning came we looked like the imaginary Adam 'of the earth' so completely were we encased in dust."

As the Confederates moved into position to launch their attacks, McPherson was busy adjusting his lines. The general was concerned about the delicate position of his vulnerable left and so was Frank Blair, whose *XVII Corps* commanded that section of the line. During the twenty first, Blair extended his line south and strengthened his position with entrenchments and abatis. The next day, McPherson sent Dodge's *XVI Corps* to support Blair as a precaution against any Rebel attack on the left. Originally, Dodge's men had been detailed to complete the destruction of the Georgia Railroad at Decatur, but McPherson convinced Sherman that the force could be better utilized on the Federal left. Dodge's corps fortuitously arrived to the east of Blair, facing

Debris left over from the grim contest of the battle of Atlanta. The Confederates lost 8,000 men during the contest while Sherman's army suffered 3,300 casualties during the battle.

Major General William H. T. Walker, a divisional commander in Hardee's Corps killed in the early moments of the battle of Atlanta on 22 July 1864.

south, in a perfect position to meet Hardee's attack when it finally came.

Meanwhile, to the south of McPherson's position Hardee was encountering vexing difficulties in positioning his troops to launch the attack. The march was already several hours behind schedule and the general was unsure of the exact position of McPherson's line. When he turned north to advance on the assumed location of the *Army of the Tennessee*, he had Cleburne's Division take the left while Walker's, Bate's and Maney's were stretched out to the right. The advance had to cover a large stretch of terrain that played havoc with the Confederate ranks. Thick woods, ravines and swamps disjointed the lines, breaking them apart into confused masses of men. Another problem arose when W. H. T. Walker's Division found its advance blocked by a large mill stream. The frustrated division commander approached Hardee to describe his situation, but only won a harsh rebuke from the general, who was growing steadily more irritated by the day's turn of events. Incensed by Hardee's acerbic remarks, Walker turned to a staff officer and growled, "I shall make him remember this insult. If I survive this battle he shall answer me for it." Difficulties continued when Maney's division accidentally broke off from the rest of the advancing corps. Instead of delaying the advance further to allow the command to return to its original position in line, Hardee was forced to place the misguided division with Cleburne, on the left. It was a badly disheartened and disorganized corps that finally advanced to make the critical attack against the Federals on 22 July.

When the Confederates finally did reach the Federal line after 1200, they found themselves not on the flank or in the rear of enemy's position as had been supposed, but almost squarely in front of a division of Dodge's corps under General Sweeny. Picket fire broke out as the Southerners closed on the National line. Dodge heard the shots in front of Sweeny's division and quickly began to respond to the impending attack. The corps commander ordered Fuller's division to go into position between Sweeny's and Blair's commands. Rather than command the fight from the rear, Dodge chose to remain at the front with his men, directing regiments as if he were a brigade commander. The picket fire increased incrementally to eventually become massive discharges by the time Walker's and Bate's divisions moved forward against Dodge. As the fight grew, General Walker was among the first Confederates to fall. Killed by a Federal minie ball, the general would lost forever the chance to win redress from Hardee. Finally, the Confederate line emerged from the woods in Dodge's front and charged against the Bluecoats. Walker's and Bate's Confederates rushed 300 yards under a devastating fire, over mostly open ground, for the Federal line. Although they managed to close in to within a few yards of the Federals, the men in Butternut were repulsed with heavy casualties. Undaunted, the Rebels redressed their lines and charged forward again as Federal cannon fire cut bloody gashes in their ranks. One Yankee recalled:

> Picket's famed charge could not have been braver or more desperate, and I may add more signally repulsed. It became impossible to withstand the leaden rain of our infantry and the iron hail of our batteries, and when they had reached the center of the open ground in our front, the columns were broken and thrown into great confusion.

Swept from the Federal front by the horrific fire, Walker's and Bate's divisions retreated for safety. One Federal commander would later remark, "The Lord put

A romantic interpretation of the death of Major General James B. McPherson after he was shot by Confederate troops during the battle of Atlanta on 22 July 1864. McPherson was the only Federal army commander killed in action during the Civil War.

Dodge in the right place today."

Cleburne's Division enjoyed considerably more success, sweeping through a gap between Dodge and Blair. In the process the Confederates managed to take the life of one of the Union's most promising generals; James B. McPherson. McPherson had been conferring with Sherman when Hardee's attack finally got under way. Concerned about his left flank, McPherson hurriedly rode off to investigate Dodge's situation. Once satisfied that Dodge was holding his own, McPherson headed west with his staff for Blair's section in the line, only to stumble accidentally into Cleburne's advancing Confederate troops. Spotting the general, Confederate Captain Richard Beard raised his sword and called for his surrender. Rather than meekly accept capture, McPherson turned his horse about, raised his hat "as if he were saluting a lady," and attempted to gallop off to safety. The Southern troops fired, and a bullet found McPherson's heart. Reaching the fallen general, Beard asked a wounded orderly beside the body, "Who is this lying here?" The man replied with tears in his eyes, "Sir, it is General McPherson. You have killed the best man in our army." McPherson's body was later recovered by the Federals and brought to Sherman's headquarters. Logan was given command of the *Army of the Tennessee* in McPherson's stead, while Brigadier General Morgan L. Smith took command of the *XV Corps*.

Cleburne attempted to exploit the gap he had found by turning to the left and rolling up the Federal flank. His advance was poised to fall on Blair's extreme left, held by Brigadier General Giles A. Smith's division and Legget's division on Smith's right. Brigadier General Daniel C. Govan's brigade and Brigadier General J. A. Smith's brigade caught Giles Smith's division in the front and left, causing the unit to collapse and hundreds of panic-stricken Federals to flee for the rear. One Federal noted of the rout of Smith's men,

> Such numbers of the Fourth Division crowded the Second Brigade [Colonel Robert K. Scott's of Legget's division], or swept along its entrenchments, that it seemed the rest must be either killed or captured, especially when right behind came the rebel columns in good order....

Another Yankee remarked, "For a time it looked more like a rout than a battle." The Federals tried to send up artillery to force the Confederates back, but these were entangled in a mass of their retreating comrades and the advancing Confederate troops. Cleburne's men even captured one six-gun battery, sent to stem the Confederate advance as they continued to surge forward.

Eventually, Cleburne's attack took him along the same path as the Federals had followed to attack Bald Hill or Legget's Hill, during the previous day's fight. The prominence was held by Brigadier General Manning Force's brigade. They had helped to take the hill on the twenty-first and were just as ill-disposed to lose it as Cleburne's men were eager to retake it in order to redeem their honor. The Yankees calmly turned around to face the threat to their rear and let go a devastating small arms fire while artillery blasted away with grapeshot and canister. The Confederates charged, were repulsed, and charged again, with as little effect as before. Although the Rebels had help from Maney's Brigade, and caught Force's brigade in a pocket of fire on his front,

The site of Major General McPherson's death on the field of the battle of Atlanta McPherson's body was later recovered and brought to Sherman's headquarters where the commanding general supposedly wept over the sight of his dead friend.

Elements of the XV Corps engaged in repelling the Confederate attack on Bald Hill on 22 July. The fighting at Bald Hill was the bitterest of the battle of Atlanta.

left and rear, the Federals managed to hold on to their hill. Force himself was knocked out of the fight by a bullet in his face, but survived the awful wound.

Cleburne was eventually forced back by Federal reinforcements and those of Giles Smith's division who had remained on the field after most of the command had been routed. The new line bent back at Legget's Hill, in a 90 degree angle to the east. Troops quickly scrambled to dig in and entrench the new line using whatever implements they could lay their hands on, bayonets, knives and tin plates. Fences were torn apart and the rails used for breastworks.

Sherman had grown concerned about the dangerous situation that his army was in, but was disposed to let the *Army of the Tennessee* fight on its own, without help from any of the other forces of his command. The general later gave his reasons in his memoirs:

> I purposely allowed the Army of the Tennessee to fight this battle almost unaided...because I knew that the attacking force could only be a part of Hood's army, and that, if any assistance were rendered by either of the other armies, the Army of the Tennessee would be jealous. Nobly did they do their work that day, and terrible was the slaughter done to our enemy, though at a sad cost to ourselves....

When Logan reported that he was fighting practically the entire Confederate army and under heavy pressure, Sherman merely replied, "Tell General Logan to fight 'em, fight 'em, fight 'em like hell!"

During the course of the battle, Hood looked on from Atlanta. Instead of coordinating his planned attacks, he let Hardee's troops advance and spend themselves

Yankees of Brigadier General John W. Fuller's division of the XVI Corps rally against an attack by Hardee's Corps during the battle of Atlanta.

against the Federal position without offering any aid. Not knowing that the high water mark of Hardee's attack had already passed, Hood then ordered Cheatham to join the fray, unsupported between 1500 and 1600.

Cheatham's right division, under Major General C. L. Stevenson, advanced against Legget's Federals who had just repulsed the attack in their rear. These Yankees now turned to face towards Atlanta once more, in order to meet the new attack. The Confederates savored a few moments of victory when they successfully managed to carry a section of the Union works. However, they took an increasing number of casualties under a harsh fire from their foe and were forced to retreat from their gains.

Another of Cheatham's divisions under Brigadier General John C. Brown managed to attain a major success against the Federal right occupied by Brigadier General Morgan L. Smith's division of Logan's *XV Corps*. The Confederates of Brigadier General Arthur Manigault's brigade were able to get in close against the National troops, using a railway cut and a large house to cover their advance. When up against the Federal line, Manigault's men burst a hole in the Northern position and poured through it with elements of the rest of Brown's Division. In the process, the Rebels captured four twenty pound parrots of Captain Francis DeGress' battery of the *1st Illinois Artillery* and turned the guns on the Yankees. Four Federal brigades fled from the field, and all of a sudden there was a gaping hole of half a mile in the *XV Corps*. Logan rode to an officer during the breakthrough and shouted, "What the hell does

One of the most talented of the infamous class of political generals, Major General John A. Logan.

this mean?" When the officer informed him of the situation, Logan fumed, "Those works must be taken or the Army of the Tennessee is gone to hell." To stem the tide, Sherman brought up a battery from Schofield's *Army of the Ohio*, the only assistance from an outside force that the *Army of the Tennessee* accepted on the twenty-second. The fire from the guns, combined with rallied troops and reinforcements, forced the Rebels to retreat.

By 1700, Cheatham's attack had been thrown back and the entire Confederate offensive was in jeopardy. Cleburne and Maney attempted once more to attack the Federal left near Legget's Hill, but were repulsed again after a bout of heavy hand to hand fighting. At one point during the close combat, Colonel W. W. Belknap of the *15th Iowa* managed to grab Colonel Harris Lampley of the 45th Alabama and drag him into Federal lines shouting, "Look at your men! They are all dead!" One Federal remembered of the scene around Legget's Hill, which had been the site of attacks all day, "The dead rebels lay about as thick on one side of the works as the other, and right up to them."

The action then petered out in the darkness, with thousands of troops lying dead,

The Battle of Atlanta Cyclorama

During the mid- to late-1800's, cycloramas came into the height of their vogue. Cycloramas were huge paintings, some 50 feet high and 400 feet long, meant to completely encircle the entranced viewer, naturally overwhelmed by the experience. The themes for such massive displays varied, but by far the most popular subjects were epic military battles. Hundreds of visitors would flock to an exhibition to get a look at these marvelous spectacles.

After the Civil War, various painters were contracted to construct cycloramas depicting the great battles fought during the conflict. A French artist, Paul Philippoteaux, constructed a cyclorama of Picket's Charge which is probably the most famous of this type of painting. Another work was constructed by German artists to depict one of the greatest episodes of the Atlanta campaign, the battle of Atlanta.

The cyclorama of the battle of Atlanta was constructed by William Wehner, a German painter who established his studio called the American Panorama Company, in Milwaukee, Wisconsin in 1883. To help him in his American venture, Wehner enlisted the help of numerous German artists who had worked on cycloramas commemorating the teutonic victories of the Franco-Prussian War. One of the first great projects of the American Panorama Company was a massive depiction of the battle of Missionary Ridge. Wehner's next major project on the Civil War was to be on the battle of Atlanta.

In 1883, legend has it that former Major General John A. Logan approached Wehner to create a painting of the battle of Atlanta, a fight in which the retired soldier had played a prominent part. The work, publicized as "Logan's Great Battle," was supposedly meant to bolster the veteran's political fortunes as he ran for vice-president with Republican presidential candidate James G. Blaine in the election of 1884. The painting clearly did not have the desired impact, for the Blaine ticket lost to Democrat Grover Cleveland.

Regardless of the consequences of the election, Wehner and the artists of his American Panorama Company diligently applied themselves to the creation of a spectacular and meticulously accurate rendition of the battle of Atlanta. Ten painters were employed to labor on the subject and were divided into three categories: landscape painters, figure painters and animal painters. To insure the veracity of the work, Wehner enlisted the aid of Theodore Davis, a sketch artist for *Harper's Weekly* who had accompanied Sherman's army during many of the great battles of the Atlanta campaign. Davis had already served as a technical advisor to the Missionary Ridge project and was well suited to assist with this one as he was quite familiar with the ground on which the contest had been fought. Wehner also sent artists to Atlanta to study the terrain and make sketches of the area. Veterans and civilians appeared more than happy to assist in the quest for accuracy, approaching the German painters to give details and their reminiscences of the battle.

Though Wehner's artists succeeded in creating a masterwork of documentary painting, the cyclorama suffered a troubled history. Finally completed in 1886; the massive work, some 42 feet tall, 358 feet in circumference and weighing 9,334 pounds, vividly portrayed the breakthrough and repulse of Maginault's brigade of Confederates on the Federal right, as well as a variety of other episodes which took place on the grim day of 22 July. It first went on exhibition at Detroit and then was displayed at Minneapolis and Indianapolis. Later, due to legal difficulties, the painting had to be sold. A purchaser acquired the work in 1892 and displayed it in a huge drumlike structure in Atlanta. In January 1893, the cyclorama suffered damage when a large snowfall caused the roof of the exhibition building to collapse. Worse still, the number of visitors who came to see the painting dwindled so much that it had to be auctioned off, fetching $1,100. Fortunately, the painting was bought up by a philanthropist who then sold the work to the city of Atlanta, in 1898.

Since then the painting has undergone numerous alterations. In 1935-1936, a WPA grant funded the creation of a diorama at the base of the painting to give it a three dimensional effect. Included in the model are cannons, trees, railroad tracks and 128 figures of Union and Confederate soldiers. The artists who worked on the project paid homage to actor Clark Gable, of *Gone with the Wind* fame by adding a figure that bears a striking resemblance to the actor. In 1979, the painting was closed to the public for a massive $11,000,000 restoration effort, which took three years. Today, the cyclorama can be seen in its full glory in a 200-seat revolving theater with lighting and sound effects.

Confederates of Brigadier General Arthur Manigault's Brigade attempt to hold their gains in the face of a powerful Yankee counter attack. Manigault's brigade managed to capture a battery of Federal guns when it broke through the line of the XV Corps, but was eventually forced to retreat.

dying or wounded on the bloody field of the battle of Atlanta. All Hood could do was withdraw his battered forces into the works around the city the next day. Once again, Hood's assault had been disorganized, and launched piecemeal and unsupported. The Army of Tennessee had suffered an enormous loss of some 8,000 men during the day, for no purpose or gain. Sherman sustained less than half as many casualties. Given the failure of the offensive, Hood decided to wait for Sherman to make the next move.

The Badge of the *XV Corps*

The unit patch, one of the American military's greatest traditions, was initiated during the Civil War. The practice was the brainchild of Brigadier General Philip Kearny. While a divisional commander in the *Army of the Potomac* during the Peninsular Campaign, Kearny stumbled on a group of officers, supposedly from his command, idly standing by the side of a road. The general approached the gathering and berated them for their criminal inactivity, only to discover, to his embarrassment that they were not even from his command. To avoid a repeat of such an occurrence, Kearny had his men wear a red diamond patch on their caps to distinguish them from the soldiers of other commands. Later, the practice was adopted by other units. In 1863, Major General Daniel Butterfield devised a system using a different patch for each corps of the *Army of the Potomac*. Eventually the practice caught on in the West as well. A Captain C. W. Pepper recounted the story of how the *XV Corps* of the *Army of the Tennessee* settled on its badge in his "Personal Recollections."

An Irish soldier of the 15th Corps came by the headquarters of General Daniel Butterfield at Chattanooga. He was a tired and weather-beaten straggler, one of those who made Sherman's march from Memphis to Chattanooga, thence to Knoxville, and was returning in the cold of that march from Knoxville to Chattanooga. He was thinly clad, one foot covered with a piece of rawhide bound with strings about a sockless foot. "Arms at will," he trudged past the headquarters guard intent only on overtaking his regiment.
"Halt," said a sentinel with a bright gun, clean uniform and white gloves.
"What do you belong to?"
"Eighth 'Misshoory', sure."
"What division?" "Morgan L. Smith's, av coorse."
"What brigade?"
"Giles Smith's, second brigade of the second division."
"But what army Corps?"
"The Fifteenth, you bloody fool, I am one of the heroes of Vicksburg. Anything more, Mr. Sentinel?"
"Where is your badge?"
"My badge is it, what is that?"
"Do you see this star on my cap? That is the badge of the 12th Corps. The crescent on my partner's cap is the badge of the 11th Corps."
"I see, now. That's how yez Potomick fellers git home ov dark nights. Ye takes the moon and stars with ye."
"But what is the badge of your corps?"
Slapping his cartridge box the soldier replied:
"D'ye see that? A cartridge box, with a U.S. on a brass plate and forty rounds in it, and sixty rounds in out pockets; that's the badge of the 15th Corps that came from Vicksburg to help you fight at Chattanoogy."
It is said that when Logan heard of this incident, he adopted the cartridge box, with the inscription 'Forty Rounds' as the badge of the 15th Corps.

CHAPTER XII

EZRA CHURCH

23 July - 28 July, 1864

Sherman had successfully fielded two of Hood's offensives and had rewarded the Confederates with heavy casualties for his bravado. However, the Confederates were still safely tucked away in their extensive network of entrenchments protecting Atlanta. For a short period after the 22 July, both Sherman and Hood rested their forces and sought replacements for the general officers who had so far been lost during the battles around Atlanta. The respite from battle was to be a short one, for Sherman was once again on the move to sever the city's rail links. At the same time, Hood was ever watchful for another opportunity to strike.

Sherman's first major act after the battle of Atlanta was to appoint a successor to McPherson for the command of the *Army of the Tennessee*. Sherman had a wide range of talent to draw upon for this task, including John Logan, who had performed ably in McPherson's place on the twenty-second, and Joseph Hooker, a former commander of the *Army of the Potomac*. However, after a conference with his subordinates, Sherman finally settled on Major General Oliver O. Howard. Though Howard had suffered bad luck while serving as a corps commander with the *Army of the Potomac*, he had performed ably out west and had won the respect of his fellow commanders. Nevertheless, the decision was not popular in certain quarters of Sherman's army. Logan was hurt that he was not chosen, but was professional enough not to let such ill feeling hamper his dealings with the new commander of the *Army of the Tennessee*. He remained on friendly terms with Howard, though he continued to claim that he was by-passed only because he was a citizen soldier and not a member of the elitist clique of West Point graduates which included Sherman and Howard. Hooker, on the other hand, was indignant. Not only was a junior officer being promoted over his head, but Howard had served in a subordinate position to "Fighting Joe" during the Chancellorsville campaign. Hooker complained that he had been subject to insults and indignities throughout the entire campaign, but this was the final straw. He penned his resignation to Sherman and it was quickly accepted. Sherman had no respect for Hooker's abilities and considered the general a potentially dangerous liability. The affair at Kolb's farm loomed foremost in Sherman's dislike a "Fighting

132 / THE ATLANTA CAMPAIGN

Major General William T. Sherman confers with his army commanders over his next bold move during the confrontations around Atlanta.

Joe." Yet, despite Sherman's distaste for Hooker, he was respected by his men who were displeased by his removal. One soldier of the *XX Corps* wrote:

> I do not believe that the highest officers generally sympathized with Hooker, but the corps as a whole felt that his loss was a serious blow. He had a large personal influence on his troops. During an active campaign, virtually every soldier in his corps saw him almost daily. If there was a picket line to be established, he personally examined it; if an assault was to be made on the enemy, he was with the foremost, always brave to the extreme of recklessness. He was moreover, careful of the welfare of his men....

Hooker was temporarily replaced by Alpheus Williams until Sherman's handpicked successor Major General Henry Slocum, arrived to take command of the *XX Corps*.

On 25 July, Sherman lost another general, Brigadier General Thomas W. Sweeny. Dodge and his division commanders, Sweeny and Fuller, were discussing the battle of Atlanta on that day when Sweeny vehemently accused Fuller and his men of cowardice for not properly supporting him during the fight. When Dodge tried to defend Fuller, Sweeny broke into a series of blistering insults. The Irish Sweeny was known to be unsurpassed in this field. One comrade, who knew him well, claimed that the general could speak three languages fluently: English, Irish and the profane "punctuated by exclamation points." In his rage, Sweeny yelled at Dodge, "You are a god damned liar, sir!," "You are a cowardly son of a bitch, sir!" and "You are a god damned inefficient son of a bitch, sir!" The enraged Dodge slapped Sweeny who retaliated by punching his commander in the nose with his one arm (the other had been lost to a wound during action in the Mexican War). A full scale brawl erupted, with Fuller coming to Dodge's aid. When it was finally broken up, Sweeny was put

Oliver O. Howard
1830-1909

Oliver Otis Howard was born in Maine and attended numerous schools before he graduated from Bowdoin College and then entered West Point. He left the Academy a prominent fourth in a class consisting of other notable figures in the Civil War, such as J. E. B. Stuart. Howard spent most of his pre-war days in the passive role of a mathematics professor at the Military Academy.

When the war broke out, Howard soon found himself a colonel at the head of the *3d Maine Regiment*, which he commanded during First Bull Run. Howard was promoted to brigadier general after his first major fight and saw service in the Peninsular campaign, where he lost his right arm on the battlefield of Seven Pines. The wound was not enough to keep Howard down and out for long. Three months later he was back on duty, commanding a brigade during the battle of Second Bull Run. At Antietam, Howard was commanding a brigade in Major General John Sedgwick's division when it was caught in a destructive pocket of enemy fire in the West Wood. After Sedgwick fell, wounded, Howard assumed command of the battered unit.

By the battle of Fredericksburg, Howard had been promoted to a major general in command of a division and soon thereafter attained command of the *XI Corps*. Howard's tenure in charge of

Major General Oliver O. Howard.

this unit was to be an unhappy and unlucky one. The corps achieved infamy when it was routed during a flank attack by Stonewall Jackson's troops at the battle of Chancellorsville, on 1 May. A few months later, Howard assumed command of the *I Corps* and *XI Corps* during the first day of the battle of Gettysburg, on 1 July. Though his forces were driven from the field, Howard had the foresight to set up a defensive position on Cemetery Hill which the *Army of the Potomac* would hold for the rest of the battle.

After performing competently throughout the contest at Gettysburg, Howard and his *XI Corps* were transferred west to fight at Chattanooga under Major General Joseph Hooker. With the *XI* and *XII Corps* combined into the *XX Corps* under Hooker, Howard received command of the *IV Corps* of the *Army of the Cumberland* which he would command for most of the Atlanta campaign. During Sherman's advance into Georgia, Howard won the respect of many of his fellow officers for his ability, though he was severely defeated at Picket's Mill on 27 May. When the commander of the *Army of the Tennessee*, Major General James B. McPherson, was killed during the battle of Atlanta, Sherman selected Howard to replace him. Howard would command the force until the end of the war.

Though Howard remained in the military and received the rank of regular brigadier general and brevet major general, he also concerned himself with the plight of newly freed Afro-Americans. He headed the Freedman's Bureau, organized various services for freed slaves and also fought for civil rights for blacks. Perhaps his most lasting legacy was the establishment of Howard University in Washington, D.C.

---

under arrest and later sent up to Nashville to face a court martial.

The Army of Tennessee faced some command changes as well. Lieutenant General Stephen D. Lee arrived to take command of Hood's old corps from Cheatham, who reverted back to division command. The youthful Lee, only 30 years old at the time, had seen distinguished service in the East and West and more recently had been the commander of the Department of Alabama, Mississippi, and East Louisiana before joining Hood's command.

As for the other vacancies opening up at the divisional level, Hood found a dearth of experienced commanders who could fill these positions. Thomas C. Hindman asked to be relieved due to illness and he was replaced by Patton Anderson. Since no suitable candidate existed to take the place of Walker, killed at the battle of Atlanta, his old division was broken up and detailed to Cheatham's, Cleburne's and Bate's commands.

By 27 July, Sherman was on the move, again this time across the northern face of Atlanta. Sherman's troops had significantly disrupted the Georgia Railroad and the Western & Atlantic's bridge over the Chattahoochee had been repaired, so that Sherman was receiving plenty of supplies to support his next moves. Sherman hoped to get around Atlanta by the west and cut the two remaining lines running into the city: the Macon & Western and the Atlanta & West Point. The latter had already been substantially damaged by a recent Federal cavalry raid, but it would take the destructive capacity of infantry to put both lines completely out of commission. A critical target would be the city of East Point; where both lines merged to run into Atlanta.

Sherman decided to threaten the railway by sidling around Atlanta. The *Army of the Tennessee* was to lead the move by taking a new position on the western flank of the army. On 27 July, Howard's force began moving behind the *Army of the Ohio* and *Army of the Cumberland* to arrive on the Federal right and extend the flank out so as to threaten the common track from East Point. While the *Army of the Tennessee* was on the move, Sherman also decided to employ his cavalry in a raid against the Atlanta & West Point and the Macon & Western railroads. The attack took the form of two columns. One, under Brigadier General Edward M. McCook, was to sweep down around the west of Atlanta onto the Atlanta & West Point, and then to proceed east, to hit the Macon & Western between Lovejoy's Station and Jonesboro. Major General George Stoneman and Brigadier General Kenner Garrard were to pass around the eastern face of Atlanta to join up with McCook, in order to destroy the Macon & Western. Stoneman also won permission to head south once he had crippled the railroad, to free Federal prisoners of war held at Macon and Andersonville.

As Sherman got under way with his multiple movements, Hood was planning to hit the Federals with another grand flanking maneuver plagiarized from General Lee. This time the major objective was the Federal right. Hood knew Sherman was

Site of one of the bloodiest battles during the Atlanta campaign, Ezra Church.

planning to hit the Confederate rail links and planned to stop his advance by having Lee's Corps seize the crossroads of the Lick Skillet Road and Marietta Pike at Ezra Church, to block their path. With the Federals stymied at Ezra Church, Stewart's command was to advance behind Lee's command, swing around that corps' left, and hit the Nationals in flank.

Unfortunately for Hood, the Federals reached the crossroads first. On 28 July, Howard positioned the *Army of the Tennessee* on the right of the *Army of the Cumberland* to command the vital crossroads at Ezra Church. This extended the Federal lines two miles to the south west. The Federals expected that the move might draw Hood to make a flank attack, and so the *Army of the Tennessee* prepared for the hostilities by digging in. The Federal line extended south in the shape of a fish hook, with Blair's *XVII Corps* faced east on the left while Logan's *XV Corps* held the right. Logan's command was set up so that Brigadier General Charles R. Woods division was on the left, facing east, while Giles Smith's division was refused towards the west, facing south to protect against any flank attack. In entrenching, the Federals used whatever implements they could to solidify their position. One Federal brigade impiously appropriated the pews of Ezra Church for breastworks.

Lieutenant General Stephen D. Lee had moved out for Ezra Church at 1000 on 28 July, only to find, to his consternation, that the Federals had beaten him there, entrenched, and were in command of the vital crossroads. Believing that the Federals had just arrived on the field, the young Confederate commander felt that a powerful attack would drive them from their advantageous position.

The Confederate attack began with Major General James C. Brown's Division of Lee's Corps attempting to drive up against Smith's part of the line on the Federal right. Logan stood with his well-entrenched troops waving his sword and shouting words of encouragement as the first attack came. Brown's Division drove in the Federal pickets but was devastated by a hail of fire from the Bluecoats. The attack wavered and then was forced to retreat by a Federal counterattack. Brown committed his reserves and attempted to push forward again, only to meet failure once more. After suffering a heavy loss of 800 casualties and three brigade commanders, Brown gave up smashing his ranks against the Federal's strong position.

Once Brown had started to receive this rough handling in front of the Federal lines, Lee committed Major General H. D. Clayton's Division. Through an error, one of Clayton's brigades, under Brigadier General Randall Gibson, attacked prematurely, without the support of the rest of the division. Gibson's men surged forward with elan to strike Colonel Hugo Wangelin's brigade of Logan's corps holding the angle in the Union fishhook line. The Confederates attempted to drive Wangelin's men from their breastworks of pews, but were unable to make any significant headway. Clayton's second brigade, under Brigadier General Alpheus Baker, then entered the fray against Wangelin's brigade, only to be brushed off with a blizzard of musketry. Both of Clayton's brigades had lost some 50 percent of their number as casualties in these fruitless attacks.

Despite his heavy losses and significant repulses, Lee was still convinced that the Federals had only just arrived on the field and were not firmly entrenched. Thus, when Stewart's Corps began arriving on the battleground, Lee incautiously decided to commit these troops to the action. Major General E. C. Walthall's command was the first of Stewart's divisions to arrive and was thrown into battle against the Federal right, over the same ground that Brown had covered earlier.

The profane Irishman who let his temper get the best of him, Thomas W. Sweeny.

Major General Grenville M. Dodge.

Sherman's Great Cavalry Raid

On 27 July, Sherman launched a grand cavalry movement against the Macon & Western Railroad. Sherman conceived two great damaging thrusts to accomplish in order to threaten his enemy's ability to hold Atlanta. One force of 3,500 men, led by Brigadier General Edward M. McCook, was to head around the western face of Atlanta to fall upon the line at Lovejoy's Station, 22 miles south of the city. Another force of 6,500 men, under Major General George Stoneman and Brigadier General Kenner Garrard, was to head around the town to the east and to join McCook at Lovejoy's Station in the destruction of the line. On 26 July, General Stoneman asked Sherman for permission to extend the purpose of the raid. He put forth an ambitious plan to head further south for Macon after he had accomplished his destructive work at Lovejoy's Station. There, he would free 1,500 Federal officers held in a prison. Once this task was achieved, Stoneman's troopers would head southwest for Andersonville, to free the 30,000 prisoners held in abominable conditions at Camp Sumter amid disease and suffering. Sherman remarked of Stoneman's objectives, "This is probably more than he can accomplish, but it is worthy of a determined effort."

On 27 July, the Federal cavalry began its raid. McCook advanced south along the west bank of the Chattahoochee, crossed the river below Campbellton, and fell upon the Atlanta & West Point Railroad at Palmetto. There McCook's troopers destroyed what they could, including a depot, telegraph poles, bales of cotton and freight cars loaded with food and supplies. From Palmetto, the Federals headed east and took a supply depot at Fayetteville, where they destroyed tents, wagons and supplies as well as capturing 300 surprised Confederates. To their delight, the Federals also commandeered thousands of dollars in Confederate scrip from a Confederate paymaster.

By 0700, McCook's men had finally arrived on the Macon & Western at Lovejoy's Station and set to work destroying the line while awaiting the arrival of Stoneman. At least two miles of track were pulled up and destroyed, and cars containing a variety of stores were burned. However, instead of Stoneman's troops, Confederate cavalry appeared, and McCook decided to make a hasty retreat west. The Federal cavalry was hit around Fayetteville but continued west, encountering more Confederate cavalry at Newnan. McCook's command was routed in a battle there and sent fleeing for Marietta. McCook had not managed to do much lasting damage in the Confederate rear, but he had caused the Rebels some concern.

While McCook suffered a repulse, Stoneman rode into a major disaster. When Stoneman advanced from Decatur on 27 July, he split up his force, sending Garrard with 4,300 of his troops to occupy Wheeler's cavalry force. Stoneman then flagrantly disobeyed his instructions and took the rest of his command off to the southeast to attack the Macon & Western east of Macon, between Gordon and Griswold Station.

The cavalry movement soon ran into serious difficulties. Garrard encountered a large number of Wheeler's troopers ten miles south of Decatur and decided to retreat north. Meanwhile Stoneman was on the Macon & Western, damaging the line as he moved east towards the city of Macon. On 30 July, the Federal cavalry began shelling the town, throwing its citizens into a panic, but found it safely defended by Georgia Militia under Howell Cobb. Stoneman then decided to abandon his grandiose plans of liberating Federal prisoners and headed north towards Athens and safety. The next day, at Sunshine Church near Round Oak, Stoneman was trapped and surrounded by cavalry belonging to Brigadier General Alfred Iverson's mounted brigade. Iverson had cleverly managed to dupe Stoneman into believing that the Confederates had a larger force than was actually present. The Federal general surrendered, but was able to sneak away two brigades which continued north. The Confederates proceeded to plague the Federals as they attempted to escape and enjoyed a sharp fight at Jug Tavern, west of Athens, on 3 August. The remnants of Stoneman's Federal command were broken up and left riding for safety in a panic. The next day, 400 survivors of Stoneman's disastrous expedition rode into Marietta with news of what had occurred.

The entire raid had been a costly and embarrassing failure. All in all, Sherman lost 4,200 troopers during this escapade, almost half of his entire cavalry force. Angered by this outcome, Sherman became convinced that cavalry would be unable to damage the remaining Confederate rail lines sufficiently. Instead, his infantry would have to force its way around the enemy army in order to destroy the Atlanta & West Point and the Macon & Western.

A Confederate wagon train stationed at Fayetteville, Georgia becomes prey for Federal cavalry under Brigadier General Edward M. McCook during his raid south of Atlanta.

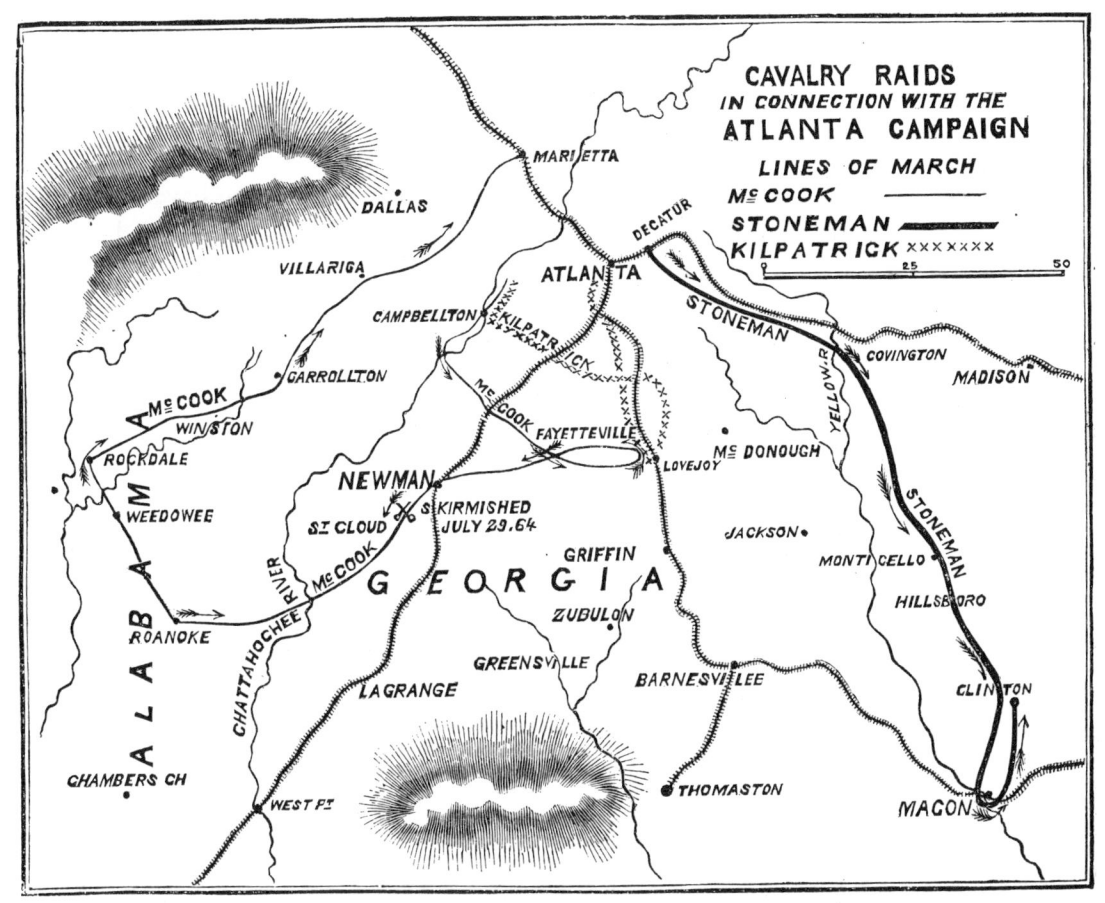

Behind the Federal lines, Oliver O. Howard was ably leading the *Army of the Tennessee* in his first battle as an army commander. Howard had reason to be somewhat concerned about his right, as the Confederates continued to drive against his line. Jefferson C. Davis' division was supposed to have been sent from Thomas' army to protect the flank of the *Army of the Tennessee*, but it had not yet arrived on the field. Howard therefore decided to strengthen the flank with regiments from Dodge and Blair as well as 26 artillery pieces. These were all in position to meet Walthall's men when they attacked.

As Walthall pressed up against the Yankee position held by Smith's brigades, he ran into the same deliberate and destructive fire that had torn apart earlier Confederate attacks. Walthall's command was slaughtered in great numbers but drove to within 25 yards of the Northern line before collapsing under the fire and fleeing from the field. One Georgia colonel cried out to his retreating soldiers to ask why they were running. "Because I kaint fly!" came the reply from one southerner. Walthall claimed to have lost 152 officers and 1,000 men, almost a third of his force. Around 1600, Stewart was struck on the forehead by a bullet as he directed Loring's Division to cover the retreat of Walthall's devastated command. Loring also fell wounded during the fray. Walthall then took command of the bloodied and battered corps. By 1800, the Confederates had fallen back to safety.

Ezra Church proved to be the bloodiest one sided blunder of the Confederate leadership. Around 3,000-5,000 troops had been lost in Lee's costly assaults against Howard's line while the Federals only suffered around 600 casualties. One Federal from the *105th Illinois* wrote of the battle:

> We whipped them awfully. Their dead they left almost in line of battle along our entire front of two divisions....I am tired of seeing such butchery, but if they charge us that way once a day for a week, this corps will end the war in this section.

Another Federal wrote that the number of dead so thickly covered the field of battle that in certain places it was possible to walk on the bodies without touching the ground. Since the Confederates never asked for a truce to bury their dead, the Federals lined up Butternut corpses and covered them with a light sheet of dirt. This dusting was washed away during the next rain, leaving a grisly and ghastly sight.

Brigadier General Charles R. Woods' division of the XV Corps destroys a ill-fated charge by Brigadier General H. D. Clayton's Division of Rebels at Ezra Church on 28 July 1863.

Stephen D. Lee
1833-1908

One of the youngest Civil War generals on either side was Stephen D. Lee, a distant relation of the renowned Robert E. Lee. After graduating from West Point in 1854, Lee was employed in the artillery and staff in positions before he went south in February, to join the Confederate armed forces.

At first, the young general saw distinguished service as a staff officer to Pierre Toutant Beauregard during the bombardment of Fort Sumter, and in command of the artillery of Lieutenant General James Longstreet's Corps during the battles of Second Bull Run and Antietam. Lee was then transferred out West, were he oversaw the defeat of Major General William Tecumseh Sherman's attempt to move on Vicksburg at Chickasaw Bayou. During the rest of the Vicksburg campaign in spring and early summer of 1863,, Lee served as a major

Lieutenant General Stephen D. Lee

general under Lieutenant General John C. Pemberton as Major General Ulysses S. Grant swept down and took the city and its garrison. Captured at Vicksburg, Lee was later exchanged and returned to command.

Promoted to major general in late 1863, Lee commanded cavalry in Mississippi and Alabama, and the Department of Alabama, Mississippi and East Louisiana. In June 1864 he was promoted to Lieutenant General and given a corps command in the Army of Tennessee. The young general led the corps it during the serious defeats of Ezra Church and Jonesboro. He later accompanied his commander, General John B. Hood, on the disastrous Nashville campaign. Lee was wounded after the collapse of the Army of Tennessee at Nashville and returned to field command only shortly before the Confederate surrender in 1865.

After the war, Lee adopted Mississippi as his home state. He engaged in agriculture and state politics and was the first president of the Mississippi Agricultural and Mechanical College.

However, some Yankees treated the Confederate dead with respect. A Southern color bearer, who had been shot down after carrying his standard to within a few feet from the Federal line was given a proper burial, with a marker noting his name and unit and telling of his last deed of valor. The Confederates were demoralized by the defeat, the leader who had mishandled the battle, and the amount of casualties that had been suffered. Some described it as "disappointing," others called it "disgusting." When a Federal called out to the Southern lines after the battle, "Say, Johnny. How many of you are there left?" a Rebel replied, "Oh about enough for another killing." Lee blamed the loss on the timidity of his troops, believing that the soldiers of the Army of Tennessee cowered when put before enemy trenches and works, and refused to

The high watermark of the Confederate attack at Ezra Church. Though the Southerners managed to press within 25 yards of the Federal line in some places, the attack was torn apart by Yankee musketry and artillery.

140 / THE ATLANTA CAMPAIGN

attack with the utmost elan needed to achieve victory.

After achieving a great win at Ezra Church, Sherman decided to wait for the results of his cavalry raid. Over the next few days, the disappointing news slowly arrived at Federal headquarters: Stoneman's column had been all but crushed, Garrard's force had barely gotten off before it was repulsed by Confederate cavalry, and McCook's command managed to do a modicum amount of damage before being driven away in retreat. If the railroads were to be destroyed now and his victories around Atlanta truly to account for something, infantry would have to do the job.

Federal infantryman Harry Davis takes the colors of the 30th Louisiana lost on the field of Ezra Church.

Casualties of the Confederate attack at Ezra Church. Hood lost up to 5,000 men during the battle while inflicting only minor casualties.

CHAPTER XIII

UTOY CREEK TO JONESBORO

29 July - 1 September, 1864

For several weeks after Ezra Church, the Union army stood stymied before the city of Atlanta. Hood had given up his aggressive attempts to force Sherman back from the city and engaged in a more passive, but more successful policy of merely blocking Sherman's army from the Confederate supply lines. However, the wily Federal commander eventually undertook one of the most daring moves of the entire campaign, catching the Confederates off guard and making Atlanta almost completely untenable.

After his victory at Ezra Church, Sherman had decided to continue shifting his forces to the right to threaten Atlanta's remaining railroads. On 2 August, Schofield's *Army of the Ohio* was pulled from the left flank, around the rest of the army, and then positioned on the right flank. When Schofield completed the movement the next day, the Federal line then extended a mile south to North Utoy Creek and was at least two miles away from the common line of the Macon & Western and Atlanta & West Point railroads.

Two days after Schofield moved to the Federal right, Sherman was ready to have the *Army of the Ohio* press forward to take East Point. Sherman detailed Palmer's *XIV Corps* of the *Army of the Cumberland* to serve under Schofield's direction to support the intended assault. Unfortunately for the Federals, the attack was unnecessarily delayed by a silly argument over seniority between the commander of the *XIV Corps*, Major General Palmer, Schofield and Sherman. Palmer rejected Sherman's orders arguing that he was Schofield's superior by virtue of an earlier commission as major general. Sherman responded by pointing out that Schofield and Palmer were commissioned as major generals the same day, allowing Schofield's earlier commission as brigadier general to supersede Palmer's. The argument persisted for two days, with Palmer refusing to offer much help to Schofield and demanding that Sherman relieve

A Confederate fort, close-by the path of the Atlanta and West Point Railroad as it entered Atlanta, in Federal hands

him. On 6 August, Sherman accepted Palmer's resignation and placed Jefferson C. Davis in command of the *XIV Corps*.

By the time the Federals were finally able to launch an attack on East Point, they found that Hood had already reacted to block Sherman's maneuver. Bate's Division of Hardee's Corps was sent to the left on 31 July to extend Lee's line out to the South Utoy Creek. Bate had originally occupied a line 100 yards before a primary section of Confederate works built two miles from East Point to defend the railroad. Hood also had Hardee be ready to move troops to support Bate, in case the Federals managed to make any gains.

Schofield had skirmished briefly with Bate on the fifth, but on the sixth he was finally able to make the attack Sherman which had intended four days earlier. To start with, he threw Colonel James W. Reilly's brigade of Cox's division forward against Bate's Division, at 1000. Reilly's Federals encountered an entanglement of brush and timber but pressed on, only to be repulsed by a withering fire which caused 300 casualties. Schofield then attempted to flank Bate's left with Hascall's division, which succeeded in driving the Rebels back to the Confederate fortifications near to East Point. The next day, Schofield attacked these works with the *XIV Corps*, but was repulsed after suffering 200 casualties. The failure of Schofield's effort forced Sherman to seek another way to cut Atlanta's rail lines.

On 7 August, Sherman telegraphed Halleck that he was going to halt in his current position before Atlanta, at least for the moment. He ordered two 30-pound parrotts and other siege guns forward from Chattanooga to reinforce his regular artillery for a terrific bombardment of the town, in order to make it "too hot to be endured." As Sherman told Halleck,

> I am too impatient for a siege, and don't know but this is as good a place to fight it out on, as farther inland. One thing is for certain, whether we get inside Atlanta or not, it will be a used-up community when we are done with it.

Throughout August, the Federals pounded away on Atlanta destroying buildings, setting fires and killing civilians while Sherman pondered his next move.

As the Hood waited out the siege, he attended to two critical issues: lack of troops and replacements for casualties amongst his commanders. Hood's costly attacks throughout July had seriously depleted his forces. The general scoured the Confederacy for possible reinforcements but no significant number could be drawn from the other departments, themselves beleaguered by Federal advances. The Confederates were forced to scrape the bottom of the barrel. Staff officers, quartermasters and clerks were armed and sent out into the field, hospitals were searched for soldiers recovered from illness or wounds, and the governor of Georgia called for all able bodied men of his state to join the Confederate ranks. Even such extreme measures, could not raise sufficient men to replenish Hood's ranks.

Hood also had difficulty in finding replacements for his fallen division commanders, but was able to discover some suitable candidates. He filled command positions vacated by the wounding of Loring and Stewart with Brown and Cheatham, respectively. French, who had temporarily commanded Stewart's Corps after Ezra Church, was offended at being passed over by Cheatham and asked to be relieved.

French's discontent was combined with that of Hardee, who asked to be relieved due to his deteriorating relationship with Hood. Hood was increasingly critical of "Old Reliable's" ability and went as far as to blame him for the losses at Peachtree Creek and the battle of Atlanta. Irritated, Hardee applied to Bragg and Davis for a transfer. Davis refused, writing Hardee, "The country needs every effort of all her sons. You can most aid our cause in your present position; other motives will not be necessary to you." Hardee continued to petition for a transfer, but obeyed Davis' commands and stayed with the Army of Tennessee for the rest of the campaign. As the Confederates struggled to maintain the strength of their army, Atlanta began to crumble under a terrible bombardment.

An artillery piece situated behind an embrasure in the Confederate works at Atlanta.

Out in the trenches, the Confederates and Federals attempted to weather the temporary "siege" of Atlanta. The lines of both sides were actively bombarded by enemy guns, forcing soldiers to seek protection in bombproofs and trenches, and to keep vigilant for cannon blasts and incoming shells. At times, Billy Yank and Johnny Reb called informal truces to swap coffee and tobacco. The lull in activity was not to last, for Hood took the offensive once again with a daring cavalry raid.

After successfully obstructing the Federals west of Atlanta, Hood decided to take a costly gamble by having a large portion of his cavalry, under Wheeler, pitch into Sherman's rear. Actually, this strategy had long been a pet project of Johnston, who had called for the talented Nathan Bedford Forrest to launch a raid from Mississippi against the Federal supply lines in Tennessee. When Davis suggested Johnston use his own cavalry to launch the raid, the general flatly refused, offering a multitude of reasons. Hood was also of the opinion that the move might be risky because it would deprive him of his ability to gather intelligence on Union movements. However, he believed that the raid could ultimately result in the destruction of Sherman's supply line which would force the Federals to retreat from Atlanta in ignominy.

Hood unleashed his cavalry under Wheeler on 10 August. Despite the threat of 4,000 Southern soldiers riding into his rear, Sherman remained unconcerned and even saw the move as advantageous to the Federal cause. Sherman's nonchalant attitude stemmed from his own experiences during the campaign, which had proven that cavalry could not do enough damage to seriously impair a railroad for any length of time. All Hood had done was deprive himself of "his eyes and ears," an action Sherman that would play to his benefit.

Throughout the month of August, Wheeler attempted to wreak havoc on Sherman's supply line, but to little effect. At first he followed the Western & Atlantic up to Marietta, destroying trains and supplies. At Dalton on 14 and 15 August, he briefly threatened a garrison, retreating in the face of Federal reinforcements. He then headed up to East Tennessee where he performed some ineffectual service before heading south for safety in Alabama, on 10 September. Despite all Wheeler's activity, Sherman had not been inconvenienced in the least.

As Wheeler departed from the active theater of operations, Sherman continued to plot Hood's downfall and the seizure of Atlanta. To accomplish these objectives, the *XX Corps* was to be sent north to guard the railroad crossing over the Chattahoochee, while the rest of the army left the Federal line of communications and swung south around Atlanta, to hit the Macon & Western at Jonesboro. Sherman confided his plans in a telegraphed message to Halleck on 10 July:

> Since July 28th Hood has not attempted to meet us outside his parapets. In order to possess and destroy effectually his communications, I may have to leave a corps at the railroad-bridge, well entrenched, and cut loose with the balance to make a circle of desolation around Atlanta.

However, Sherman delayed the move to attempt another cavalry raid against the Confederate rail lines.

Sherman decided to embark on this cavalry raid, despite the failure of such moves earlier during the campaign, for two reasons. First, he was of the belief that Hood had dispatched all his cavalry against the Federal rear. Second, he finally had an aggressive cavalry commander, Brigadier General Judson Kilpatrick, in his ranks. Kilpatrick had

Joseph Wheeler
1836-1906

A native of Augusta, Georgia, Joseph Wheeler, who became known as "Fighting Joe," graduated from West Point only two years before the Civil War began. Second Lieutenant Wheeler served on the frontier during his short term of service in the Regular Army. After resigning to join the Confederacy, he was given the rank of first lieutenant in the artillery. A few months later, he had attained a colonelcy and was in command of an Alabama regiment.

While Wheeler commanded his regiment with some distinction at Shiloh, he was transferred to the cavalry, where he attained the post of chief of cavalry in Braxton Bragg's Army of Tennessee over more distinguished candidates, such as Nathan Bedford Forrest and John Hunt Morgan. After performing respectably at Perryville, Wheeler was promoted to brigadier general and saw more action at Stone's River, where his gallant deeds won him a major generalcy. When the *Army of the Cumberland* was besieged at Chattanooga during the fall of 1863, Wheeler led a spectacular cavalry raid

Major General Joseph Wheeler

which significantly damaged Yankee supply lines to that town. Wheeler's cavalry provided an irritant to Federal movements during the Atlanta campaign, but in August the cavalry commander took his forces almost entirely out of the fighting, to engage in an ineffectual raid against Sherman's rear. As a lieutenant general in the cavalry, Wheeler fought against Sherman during his Carolina campaign, but was eventually relieved, due to the lack of discipline in his command.

After the Confederacy surrendered, Wheeler was employed in politics and even in the National military. Settling in Alabama, he was elected to Congress and became chairman of the Ways and Means Committee. When the United States went to war against Spain in 1898, Wheeler took to the field under the National colors which he had once fought against, and commanded a division of dismounted cavalry. While participating in the attack on San Juan Hill, the aged solider accidentally displayed his old loyalties and shouted, "We got them damn Yankees on the run!" Though he demonstrated a lack of tactical ability by bungling the battle of Las Guasimas, Wheeler stayed in the regular army after the war as a brigadier general until his retirement in 1900.

---

just returned to the army after recovering from a wound sustained at Resaca. Upon arrival in mid-August, the cavalry general displayed his fighting spirit and fiery determination in a reconnaissance mission. Sherman was impressed by Kilpatrick's "zeal" and so employed him in the destruction of the Macon & Western Railroad.

Kilpatrick left the main army on 18 August. The next day he tore up some track on the West Point & Atlanta Railroad near Fairborn, drove off a detachment of Confederate cavalry, and moved on to Jonesboro. Arriving at the town at 1700, the Federals spent the next six hours working to destroy three miles of track and a depot. Retreating in the face of a large force of Confederate cavalry, Kilpatrick returned to Decatur on 22 August and then rejoined the rest of the army. The cavalry general proudly claimed that he had knocked out the railroad for at least ten days, only to be proved wrong by the arrival of an enemy train in Atlanta the very next day. The entire episode reinforced what Sherman already knew. As the general wrote in his memoirs, ."..I became more than ever convinced that cavalry could not or would not work hard enough to disable a railroad properly...." If Sherman was to destroy Atlanta's final rail links, he would have to employ infantry for the job.

The Railroad During the Atlanta Campaign

Perhaps the most remarkable features of the Atlanta campaign were Sherman's maintenance of his own line to support his advance and his diligence in seeing to the destruction of enemy's rail links. The danger of relying on rail transportation for operational or logistical uses lay in the vulnerability of a line to enemy attack. With Sherman's supply route hundreds of miles long and tremendously exposed to the whims of enemy raids, extensive measures were taken to protect their strategic points. Blockhouses of logs with dirt roofs and surrounded by a ditch and parapet were constructed at vital positions along the line. Each was manned by a detachment of infantry and an artillery piece. They were said to be so impregnable that only one such fort was ever captured by the Confederates during the entire Atlanta campaign.

As the Confederates retreated down the Western & Atlantic Railroad, the Federals were forced to replace and repair the destroyed track and bridges left behind by the enemy. For this task, Sherman employed a corps of talented engineers. Probably one of the most difficult jobs faced by these experts was the reconstruction of bridges destroyed in the wake of Johnston's retreat. To provide for the quick replacement of a destroyed bridge, a supply of interchangeable parts, planks and logs was stockpiled in the rear at strategic locations and rushed forward when needed. Usually, the railroad engineers completed their tasks within a few days, as if by "magic." Sherman's protection and maintenance of his own line meant that the Confederates were unable to cut him off from it for any significant amount of time.

While Sherman was well aware of the importance of his own rail lines, he was also obsessed with the idea of depriving the enemy of his support from the railroad. Sherman made sure his Federals approached the task of destroying enemy tracks with ardor, enthusiasm and an almost morbid precision. A soldier in the *105th Ohio* remembered the extensive measures which were taken:

A detachment of mounted infantry passes a blockhouse on the Nashville & Chattanooga Railroad. Blockhouses proved instrumental in protecting vital points on rail lines from attacks by Confederate guerrillas.

...the force engaged was always divided up into three bodies, with separate and distinct duties. The first marched in single file along the side of the track to be torn up, until each man stood at the end of a tie. Then, at the word of command, each stooped, took hold of the tie, and, at another word, the whole track was lifted up and overturned. Then this party marched on and renewed the movement. The second party heaped up the ties upon the track, laid the rails across them, leaving the ends extending on each side, and set the ties on fire. The third party, coming up later, took the rails, then red hot in the middle, twisted them about trees or otherwise bent and distorted them so that no rolling-mill could straighten them, wholly destroying the road for use until new ties and new rails should be supplied.

The iron rail twisted around a tree,

Yankees involved in the destruction of rails and ties. Over the course of the war, Sherman's bummers became adept in the ways of destroying railroads of the south

148 / THE ATLANTA CAMPAIGN

Troops en route from Ringgold to join Sherman's armies campaigning against Atlanta, Georgia. The Western & Atlantic Railroad served as Sherman's life line to reinforcements and supplies.

called a "Sherman's Necktie," became a symbol of the general's marches throughout the south.

Sherman's realization of the importance of the railroad, the need to protect it and to destroy the Southern access to it was an instrumental factor in the success of his campaign against Atlanta. Continuously well supplied, Sherman could continue to advance and would later be able to embark on his destructive raids throughout the South. After cutting off his enemy's rail links had been severed, there was only one unattractive choice available to the Confederates: ignominious retreat.

Brigadier General Judson Kilpatrick, Sherman's fiery cavalry commander.

The destruction of the Macon & Western Railroad between Rough and Ready and Jonesboro. With Sherman's army on Hood's last line of communication with the rest of the Confederacy, the Army of Tennessee was forced to abandon Atlanta to the Federals.

150 / THE ATLANTA CAMPAIGN

Sherman gave the orders for his grand flanking maneuver on 23 August. A week of rations were prepared for the troops, as they would be away from the regular supply lines for many days. On the night of 25 August, the *XX Corps* was sent to the Chattahoochee to guard the rail crossings over the river while the rest of the *Army of the Cumberland* pulled out of its lines to the northwest of Atlanta. The *Army of the Tennessee* moved next, and then Schofield's *Army of the Ohio*. First, the Federals stopped by the Atlanta & Western Railroad to destroy 12.5 miles of track south of East Point on 28-29 August. Sherman recalled the destruction:

> The track was heaved up in sections the length of a regiment, then separated rail by rail; bonfires were made of the ties and of fence-rails on which the rails were heated, carried to trees or telegraph-poles, wrapped around and left to cool. Such rails could not be used again; and, to be still more certain, we filled up many cuts with trees, brush, and earth, and commingled with them loaded shells, so arranged that they would explode on an attempt to haul them out the bushes.

The Federal armies approached then Macon & Western between Rough and Ready and Jonesboro. Arriving near Jonesboro about 1700 on 30 August, Howard found that a bridge over the Flint River, which ran just west of the town, had been left standing. The general quickly seized the opportunity and drove his troops over to the

Victorious elements of Brigadier General Jefferson C. Davis' XIV Corps break through the Cleburne's position on the Federal right flank at Jonesboro on 1 September 1864. The Union attack netted hundreds of Confederate prisoners including Brigadier General D. C. Govan.

east side of the river, to within rifle shot of the Macon & Western. Meanwhile Thomas' and Schofield's commands were falling on the railroad to the north. Hour by hour, Hood's last supply line was becoming increasingly endangered by the Federal advance.

When the Federals disappeared from the Rebel front on 26 August, the Confederate command was almost completely paralyzed by confusion. At first the mood in Atlanta had been jubilant, for it appeared as though Wheeler's raid had succeeded in destroying the Federal supply lines, forcing the hated Yankees to retreat. However, Hood soon began to receive uncomfortable reports that the enemy was still in the vicinity of Atlanta and up to serious mischief. On 26 August, Hardee informed Hood that Federal troops had been seen to the southwest of the city. The next day, a Confederate cavalry commander confirmed Hardee's report. By the twenty-eighth, Hood was aware of an Union force at Fairburn on the Atlanta & West Point line. Hood was unsure what exactly the Federals were up to, since Wheeler's cavalry was no longer available to give him the succinct reports on Northern activities that the general desperately needed. Suspecting a raid against the railroads in his rear, Hood dispatched two brigades of infantry to Jonesboro, and Brown's Division to Rough and Ready, on 28 August.

The next day, Hood still did not have enough information to fully divine Sherman's intentions. Reports had Sherman falling upon the Macon & Western some

point between Rough and Ready and Jonesboro. Faced with a growing threat, Hood at first acted slowly and cautiously, dispatching Hardee to Rough and Ready and Lee to East Point, on the thirtieth. Stewart's command remained in Atlanta to defend the city and possibly launch a strike into the Federal rear or flank, if the opportunity presented itself.

When Howard reached the final rail link to Atlanta, the Macon & Western, at Jonesboro and made his appearance known to the Confederates, Hood was forced to act decisively; both Hardee and Lee were ordered south to drive the Federal troops near the town into the Flint River. Hardee managed to start off south around 1600, but Lee's march was delayed for some six hours. The movement was to be a slow and painful one for the troops in Butternut. While trains were employed to shuttle the Confederates south, many had to make the long march in the heat down dusty roads. The agonizing trek was extended because the soldiers were forced to detour to the east to avoid Federal pickets north of Jonesboro. The march further depleted Confederated ranks as many troops fell by the wayside to rest rather than continue on and face battle. Hardee finally arrived at Jonesboro in the early morning of 31 August, while Lee's Corps began arriving in the area between 1100 and 1300.

With Hood remaining far from the battlefield at Atlanta, Hardee was to lead his own plus Lee's Corps, in the coming battle. Cleburne temporarily took command of Lee's Corps while Mark Lowry assumed control of Cleburne's Division. The Confederate plan was simple: Cleburne would advance his corps against Howard's right,

Federal forces engaged in destroying the Macon & Western Railroad after Hardee's forces abandoned the town.

while Lee struck the Union front.

The Federals were well placed, in a line that was almost impossible to breach. Howard's men were situated on the high ground east of the Flint River in an arc-like formation, with the *XV Corps* on the right and the *XVI Corps* on the left.

The Confederate attack was planned to open with Cleburne's assault, to be joined by Lee when he heard Cleburne's guns engaged in battle. The plan fell apart when Lee accidentally mistook picket fire from Cleburne's command for a general attack and rushed his troops forward prematurely. Lee's assault began with an artillery bombardment around 1400, and was followed by the advance of Patton Anderson's division. Anderson's men managed to get within 60 yards of Brigadier General William Harrow's division of the *XV Corps* when it was stopped cold by Yankee fire. Reinforcements were called up, but even with these the Confederates failed to take any more ground. It seemed to soldiers on both sides that the Confederates did not have full confidence in the attack. Harrow noted that the attack was not made with the Confederate's usual impetuosity. Lee bitterly recorded his disappointment with his men in his official report:

> The attack was not made by the troops with that spirit and inflexible determination that would insure success. Several brigades behaved with great gallantry, and in each brigade many instances of gallant conduct were exhibited by regiments and individuals; but generally the troops halted in the charge when they were much exposed, and within easy range of the enemy's musketry, and when they could do but little damage to the enemy behind his works in their front, instead of moving directly and promptly forward against the temporary and informidable works in their front. The attack was a feeble one and a failure with a loss to my corps of about 1,300 men in killed and wounded.

Some Confederates simply gave up and advanced on the Federal lines with their hands up, to surrender. Those who remained in the Confederate ranks retreated or were shot down.

Around 1500, Cleburne launched his attack by sending Lowry's and Brown's divisions for the Federal right held by Corse's division of the *XVI Corps*. On the advance, Lowry's Division on Cleburne's left became exposed to fire on its flank. Evidently, Lowry's men past were unaware of a cavalry force on its left flank. The commander of the detachment, the fiery Judson Kilpatrick, was both peeved and elated that he had been ignored in such a manner, as he wrote in his report: "It seemed to be the intention of the enemy to break or turn our right flank. At first he entirely ignored our command. This I determined he should not do." Kilpatrick's five regiments opened fire on the Rebels with musketry and artillery. The pestering blasts of fire and activity diverted Lowry's Division towards the west, in the direction of Kilpatrick's small force and out of the real fight against the divisions of the *Army of the Tennessee*. Meanwhile Brown's Division, which had been advancing on Lowry's right, went smack against the main Federal line, now unsupported.

The Confederates of Brown's command tramped forward against the Federals of Corse's division, ignorant of the danger they faced, with their banners floating lazily in a summer breeze. At first the Federal batteries sent out case and solid shot mercilessly smashing into the advancing Rebel ranks. As the Rebels moved closer, small arms fire picked up and began to deliver vicious blasts of musketry. As the

The destruction of Hood's ordnance train in the wake of the Army of Tennessee's retreat from Atlanta. The Confederates fired all military stores which had to be left behind in the city. A massive inferno resulted and explosions could be heard as far south as Jonesboro.

A city of the South humbled by Yankee occupation. The 2d Massachusetts Infantry's camp built next to the City Hall of Atlanta.

Confederates attempted to charge the Federal works, they plummeted into a devastating whirlwind of fire, made worse by Federal cannons now delivering blasts of double shotted canister to deadly effect. Brown's men attempted to press onward several times, but were unable to budge the Federals from their positions and thus retreated with heavy casualties.

Jonesboro turned out to be another of the painful and ill-coordinated efforts that marked battles of the Army of Tennessee during Hood's command. The battle caused 1,300 casualties in Lee's Corps and Cleburne lost some 400 troops in his failed attack. Meanwhile, the Federals had only taken a paltry 180 casualties. But the affair was not yet over, as both sides remained on the field to fight the next day.

While the Federals successfully repelled the Confederate attack at Jonesboro, the rest of Sherman's force was falling on the Macon & Western. By 1500, Schofield's *Army of the Ohio* had advanced to the rail line near Rough and Ready and proceeded to destroy its track. To the south, Major General David S. Stanley's *IV Corps* and Davis' *XIV Corps* also struck the railroad. Atlanta was now all but cut off from the rest of the Confederacy, and the Federals were in between whole parts of the Army of Tennessee, which Sherman could crush at his leisure.

The Federal commander decided to fall upon Hardee's force at Jonesboro before it could retreat or receive any help from Hood. To destroy the Rebel force, the Federal general planned to have the Schofield and Stanley fall on Jonesboro while Howard's army and Davis' division detained Hardee's troops at the town.

Meanwhile, Hood was forced to deal with an increasingly desperate situation. His forces were spread out from Atlanta to Jonesboro against a stronger enemy who was operating in his rear and severing his supply line. Throughout 31 August, Atlanta began to receive indications of an impending disaster. At 1500, Hood lost telegraphic

The effects of the Federal bombardment on the city of Atlanta. This house was in a close proximity to the Confederate entrenchments and served as a bastion for Rebel sharpshooters. It also was a favorite target for Yankee cannoneers. After Atlanta fell almost a ton of shot and shell was found in the battered structure.

contact with Hardee at Jonesboro. But word arrived that the Federals were aiming to take East Point. Erroneously assuming that the Federals were planning a primary thrust to seize Atlanta, Hood ordered Lee's Corps to move north by 0200 on 1 September. At 0100, Hardee complied with this order and sent Lee's Corps tramping north, while his own troops entrenched in anticipation for the Federal attack on the next day.

Though quick action was necessary to fall upon Hardee's exposed corps at Jonesboro, the Federal forces were slow to concentrate on the town. By 1200, only Davis' corps was in position to assist the *Army of the Tennessee* while the *Army of the Ohio* was moving south along the Macon & Western, destroying the line. Not before several hours of waiting for reinforcements could the Federals launch their attack. At 1600, the Federals of Davis' corps were assaulting Hardee's position around Jonesboro. Their target, Hardee's line, ran roughly parallel to the Western & Atlantic Railroad; his right, composed of Cleburne's Division, was refused to the right creating an angle pointing towards the north. Davis initiated the Federal attack by having Brigadier General James D. Morgan's and Brigadier General William P. Carlin's divisions attack the Confederate right where it was refused to the east. The Federals advanced into a terrible storm of musketry and canister, but managed to come within 20 yards of the Union line. However, they refused to fall back under the destructive fire and instead rallied, and charged. The troops swarmed over the Confederate entrenchments, taking 600 prisoners from Govan's Brigade, including the unit's commander. Hardee rushed reinforcements to bridge the crumbling left before a complete disaster ensued. A new line was formed only 150 yards behind the original Confederate line, blocking further Federal gains.

Sherman was elated by his success thus far at Jonesboro, but still desired a complete victory. He ordered Howard to send the *XVII Corps* around the Federal right to attack the Confederate left, and pressed Stanley to move his corps down upon the Confederate right as soon as possible. Despite Sherman's grand plans, the Federals were unable to win a decisive battle at Jonesboro. The only feat the *XVII Corps* accomplished on the first was to get over the Flint River; Stanley's corps tardily reached the field around nightfall too late to carry on the fight; and Logan's corps of the *Army of the Tennessee* was only able to engage in some light skirmishing with the Rebels. The battle closed at nightfall, with both armies still on the field. Still the Confederates had been roughly handled, losing 1,400 troops, half of which were captured in Davis' attack. The Federals suffered about the same number of casualties.

Though Jonesboro had not been a total Federal success on the field of battle, it did lead to a pair of retreats. The beleaguered Hardee was fed up with staving off large portions of the Federal army on his own and retreated south to Lovejoy's Station. Hood was also forced to depart for safety. With the rail lines around Atlanta cut, he had no option but to relinquish the town to the Yankees. The defeated troops of the Army of Tennessee left the city from 1700 to 2300 heading south to join Hardee. During the night, after the army pulled out, warehouses, supplies and the ordnance

Dejected Rebel prisoners, captured during the battle of Jonesboro are marched to the city of Atlanta also in the possession of the Federals.

train of the Army of Tennessee were fired to deny their capture by the Yankees. Throughout the early morning of 2 August, the ground around Atlanta shook from terrible explosions and the sky seared with a bloody fire and black smoke caused by the massive inferno. Atlanta had fallen.

160 / THE ATLANTA CAMPAIGN

Reward for a job well done. Federal soldiers receive their pay before they set off on the March to the Sea.

CHAPTER XIV

"ATLANTA IS OURS, AND FAIRLY WON"

September - November, 1864

Late on the night of 1 September, explosions in Atlanta could be heard by the *XX Corps* at the Chattahoochee and Sherman's forces to the south, near Jonesboro. Julian W. Hinkly of the *3rd Wisconsin Artillery* was with the *XX Corps* when the Confederates fired the stores in Atlanta. He later wrote:

> Late on the night of September first, while I was on picket duty, I heard in the direction of Atlanta what I at first thought was artillery. The rumbling kept increasing in intensity until it seemed like the heaviest firing I ever heard. Finally, a number of terrific explosions lit up the air. At six miles distance they seemed like bright flashes of lightning.

The Federals were slow to realize that Atlanta had actually fallen. At dawn on the second, Slocum advanced his command slowly towards the burnt out city. The lead column of his troops were soon met by a group of gentlemen in civilian clothing, displaying a white flag. The party included the mayor of Atlanta, James M. Calhoun, and other dignitaries who were prepared to officially surrender the city.

When Sherman heard the massive explosions wracking Atlanta, he at first thought that Hood's Confederates had attacked Slocum's *XX Corps*. The next day he learned the glorious truth. Slocum forwarded news of the capture of Atlanta to Sherman as the general was preparing to continue the campaign by following Hardee to Lovejoy's Station. As word spread, "wild hallooing and glorious laughter" was heard throughout the ranks. When Thomas learned of the news he entered into an uncharacteristic display of emotion by snapping his fingers, whistling with joy, and even almost breaking into a dance. Sherman decided that the capture of Atlanta was a sufficient prize for the time being. Instead of pursuing Hardee's force after its retreat from Jonesboro, the Federal general decided that his troops deserved a rest and thus headed north to take Atlanta, where he would plot his next move.

One of the new Federal forts guarding the city of Atlanta after its capture. In the distance is the house Hood used as his headquarters as he attempted to defend Atlanta from Sherman's advances.

Waves of joy and relief bathed the North when Sherman reported to Washington, "Atlanta is ours, and fairly won." In cities throughout the Union states, crowds celebrated the news with bands and cannon fire in honor of Sherman and his Yankee heroes. A relieved Lincoln telegraphed his thanks to Sherman and his army, while Grant rejoiced by firing a salute of double-shotted guns into the Army of Northern Virginia's entrenchments at Petersburg. The fall of Atlanta compounded other Federal victories, such as Rear Admiral David Farragut's win at Mobile Bay in early August and Major General Philip Sheridan's successful campaign against Jubal Early in the Shenandoah Valley, to strengthen the morale and the resolve of Northern soldiers and civilians who had been disheartened by the apparent lack of success in both East and West all summer.

The news was not as well received in other quarters. In the Confederacy, the fall of Atlanta was deemed a major disaster and many Rebels began to feel that defeat was now almost inevitable. Northern Democrats were also downcast by Sherman's victory. The party had delayed its national convention until late August to savor and play upon public discontent over the lack of success all summer, and exploit feelings that Lincoln's direction of the war effort had been but four years of failure. Now, as the Democratic candidate, George Brinton McClellan, accepted his party's nomination for president, victory in next election, which had once seemed so certain, appeared a faint possibility.

For several weeks after his great campaign, Sherman and his troops remained in Atlanta while the general planned his next daring move. As Sherman's army rested, its commander was once again forced to deal with logistical problems. Large stockpiles of stores needed to be amassed at Atlanta to supply the force during its stay in the city and provide for any future movements. To accomplish this task, Atlanta was to be transformed from a city into a fortified military depot that could be held by a small garrison rather than a large army. Unfortunately for the citizens of Atlanta, this course would require the retraction of the defensive works around the city, the occupation of most of the remaining buildings for military purposes, and the evacuation of the civilian population. Although Sherman realized that such measures would be unpopular, he was unconcerned. As he told Halleck in a dispatch, "If the people raise a howl against my barbarity and cruelty, I will answer that war is war, and not popularity seeking. If they want peace, they and their relatives must stop the war." Hood was notified of Sherman's intentions who responded with a harsh letter, stating:

> ...permit me to say that the unprecedented measure you propose transcends, in studied and ingenious cruelty, all the acts ever brought to my attention in the dark history of war.
>
> In the name of God and humanity, I protest, believing that you are expelling from their homes and firesides the wives and children of a brave people....

Union soldiers tear down buildings in Atlanta severely damaged by Sherman's bombardment of the town.

164 / THE ATLANTA CAMPAIGN

Atlanta in Federal hands. After taking the city, Sherman turned it into a supply depot to stockpile resources for his famous campaign through Georgia to the sea.

The Presidential Election of 1864

While the Atlanta campaign was a stunning military success, its immense political effects should not be overlooked. Sherman's victories around Atlanta, culminating in the seizure of the town, provided a desperately needed boost to Northern morale. By September of 1864, as Sherman's troops rested in the bombed and burnt out city, Northerners felt that the war finally seemed to be heading towards a conclusion, and that the triumph of Federal arms was all but certain. This feeling allowed Abraham Lincoln to win reelection in the presidential election of 1864.

Victory had not seemed all that certain in June of 1864, when Abraham Lincoln was renominated by his party to run for the presidency. Lincoln and his supporters were easily able to disarm their critics in the party, and even strengthened the presidential ticket, with a new running mate, Andrew Johnson, a War Democrat from the state of Tennessee. The policies that Lincoln and Johnson embraced during the election called for peace through the surrender or subjugation of the South and the abolition of slavery.

Obviously the major issue of the coming campaign would be the war and Lincoln's success at the polls would necessarily depend on the success of his generals on the battlefield. The Confederates were also aware of this fact. Southern generals, political leaders and citizens knew well that the survival of their infant nation depended on inflicting costly defeats on the Yankee armies when they moved to the offensive in spring of 1864. By making Northern citizens war weary through heavy casualty figures, they would hopefully induce them to bring about a conclusion to the conflict by voting for a peace candidate.

Confederate hopes rested on the success of the presidential nominee put forth by the Democrats, Lincoln's primary opposition. Democratic anti-war activists, called "Copperheads," pressed for a cessation of hostilities to engage in peace talks that would hopefully lead to reun-

A Thomas Nast cartoon entitled Dedicated to the Chicago Convention *depicting the dishonor of compromise with Jefferson Davis and the South called for by the Democratic party during the election of 1864.*

Major General, George "Little Mac" McClellan enjoying a popular welcome upon entering the city of Maryland during the Antietam campaign. Though McClellan was shelved by Lincoln in 1862, he still retained enormous popularity amongst soldiers and civilians.

ion. However, the Peace faction was counterbalanced by a block of conservative War Democrats who wanted to prosecute the war effort to restore the united country that had existed before the war, and were not interested in lofty Republican goals such as total emancipation. While both forces strove for party unity, the difference in their aims was likely to spark a fight when the party met in Chicago on 4 July to select a presidential candidate. However, events on the battlefield caused Democrats to delay their convention.

The Federal forces got under way with their multiple offensives in spring of 1864, but their lack of substantial success seemed to darken Republican hopes of holding on to the White House. Lieutenant General Ulysses S. Grant was prosecuting the war in Virginia, and suffered heavy casualties with very little to show for all the blood spilled. On 5-6 May, the *Army of the Potomac* lost 18,000 men in the battle of the Wilderness. Not long after this, another 18,000 men were lost in an almost two-week-encounter outside of Spotsylvania Court House. On a single day in June, the *Army of the Potomac* suffered 10,000 casualties in a bloody repulse at Cold Harbor. By mid-June, Grant's forces were engaged in a long and drawn out siege before Petersburg. Though Grant was winning the war, many Northern voters were asking if it was worth the cost. In the West, Sherman was actively driving back Johnston while suffering far fewer casualties than Grant. However, the relatively sluggish advance and the lack of any substantial victories did little to inspire confidence in the North, either.

As enthusiasm over the war began to plummet, the Democrats became increasingly confident in their ability to score a major victory in the fall elections.

In order to take advantage of the casualty figures from the front and the prospect of an interminable war, their convention was postponed until 29 August. However, the Democrats already had a candidate in mind for the election. Their man was the dashing and handsome Major General George Brinton McClellan. Though McClellan was a general without many battlefield successes to his credit, he was still popular amongst the Northern populace and the soldiers of the *Army of the Potomac*. After the general had been relieved from command in November of 1863, he had been courted by leading Democratic figures who were well aware of his disagreements with Lincoln over strategy and the prosecution of the war. Despite McClellan's denial of any aspirations for the presidency, it was apparent to Lincoln and the rest of the country that "Little Mac" would be nominated by the Democratic convention in late August.

As the war progressed into the sultry days of August and the new date for the Democratic convention neared, Lincoln's political fortunes appeared all but crushed by the lack of military success. Grant's campaign had thus far cost some 90,000 men and the government was calling for 500,000 more troops to be sent into action. During July and August, the National government and military was embarrassed by a Confederate raid into Maryland and Pennsylvania under Lieutenant General Jubal A. Early which almost led to the capture of Washington D.C. Sherman was still successful in the west, but no decisive victory had yet been won. The Democrats gleefully played up the issue, describing Lincoln's tenure in the presidency as "four years of failure."

Lincoln himself was pessimistic about his chances for re-election. He had already considered the necessity of abandoning abolition and negotiating with Richmond, but real proof of the president's impending sense of doom was documented by the blind memorandum which he issued on 23 August. Without allowing them to view the contents first, he asked his cabinet members to sign a document. The paper read:

> This morning, as for some days past, it seems exceedingly probable that this Administration will not be re-elected. Then it will be my duty to co-operate with the President elect, as to save the Union between the election and the inauguration; as he will have secured his election on such ground that he can not possibly save it afterwards.

While Lincoln pondered defeat and the fate of the nation, the Democrats met at Chicago. Peace and War Democrats contended to win the nomination of individuals who would propound their own agendas. While McClellan was the primary candidate, the peace faction was distrustful of the general, a known War Democrat, and looked for someone to match him. The search was in vain, for McClellan's nomination seemed unstoppable. The Copperheads were successful, however, in working their ideas into the Democratic platform. Clement Vallandigham, the foremost spokesman of the Peace Democrats, won a seat on the committee designated to write the platform. The program that was eventually written under Vallandigham's direction condemned the forcible suppression of the South and called for a cessation of hostilities, with the differences between the North and South to be discussed at a convention of states. On the thirty-first, McClellan was nominated to run on this platform in the coming presidential elections. Twenty-four hours later, McClellan's political fortunes had collapsed.

On 1 September, Atlanta fell and by the next day, was in Federal hands. The news struck the North like a thunderbolt, causing National jubilation. The victory combined with Admiral David Farragut's capture of Mobile on 5 August and Major General Philip Sheridan's victories in the Shenandoah Valley to revive Union morale. Now, the war seemed winnable as the Confederacy festered on the edge of the precipice of destruction. The victory had a definite impact on the coming elections as well. McClellan's peace platform might have seemed attractive a few days earlier, but by September it was a definite liability for it seemed to imply that the Democrats were willing to give up everything that had been gained through the bloody sacrifices of the past four years. However, McClellan was no Copperhead and did his best to disavow the platform. Unfortunately, he found himself irrevocably liked to a policy of peace before victory, or even shameful surrender.

As the election neared, Democrats attempted to seize the political initiative through a variety of tactics, including a extremely racist campaign against the Republicans. Democratic newspapers and spokesmen launched vicious printed and verbal assaults against their political adversaries, labeling them as "Black Republicans" bent on miscegenation. However, as the Federal tide of victory rolled on, the Democrats were unable to find an issue on which to successfully combat the Republicans.

By November 1864, the true death knell of the Confederacy had sounded. Lincoln was elected over McClellan by a margin of some 500,000 popular votes and 191 electoral votes. Soldiers were given absentee ballots in some states, or were "generously" furloughed by the government so that they could return home to vote. Lincoln received 119,754 votes from these fighting men, while McClellan only won 34,291 votes from the troops he once commanded. Despite McClellan's continued popularity amongst the *Army of the Potomac*, many were disillusioned by the general's association with the Copperheads and thus voted against him. Not only did the Republicans managed to capture the presidency, they also won control of statehouses in every northern state save Kentucky, Delaware and New Jersey. Furthermore, the party won a three-fourths majority in Congress. All in all, the election of 1864 was a substantially heartening triumph for Lincoln and his party.

Lincoln's victory essentially meant that the war would be prosecuted to its conclusion, and, that the South would be totally subjugated and returned to National control. The Confederates lost all hope of exhausting the North and winning a peace that might bring eventual independence. As the winter of 1864 set in, all that the Confederacy could do was wait for the inauguration of the final campaigns which would extinguish the life of their nation and bring an end to the war.

The mayor of Atlanta petitioned for Sherman's compassion, claiming that the action would cause immense suffering and untold woe. An unmoved Sherman responded to such objectives and claims by writing:

> War is cruelty and you can not refine it; and those who brought war into our country deserve all the curses and maledictions a people can pour out...You might as

Idle Federal soldiers amble along Whitehall Street in the captured city of Atlanta.

The city hall of Atlanta, Georgia.

Federals occupying what was Confederate Fort D in the entrenchments to the southwest of the city. These works were incorporated in Sherman's retracted works around the city.

well appeal against the thunder-storm as against these terrible hardships of war. They are inevitable, and the only way the people of Atlanta can hope once more to live in peace and quiet at home, is to stop the war.....

Whereas Sherman stayed at Atlanta, Hood remained inactive for most of September, but later in the month, advanced north of the Chattahoochee to get on Sherman's line of communications, in the hope of drawing the Federal general away from Georgia and back into the Tennessee River Valley. However, Sherman was not at all concerned by the Hood's movements and wrote to Grant about the threat to his lines of communication, "It will be a physical impossibility to protect the roads, now that Hood, Forrest, and the whole batch of devils, are turned loose without home or habitation." Rather than deal with Hood himself as Grant and Lincoln might have wished, Sherman sent the *Army of the Cumberland* and the *XXIII Corps* north to deal with the rampaging Confederate army while he planned to wreak such destruction on the Peach State as to make Georgia "howl." His hope was to cut the Confederacy in half again by advancing for the Georgia coast, and then to make his way north through the Carolinas for operations against the Army of Northern Virginia. Along the way, he would destroy Confederate agricultural and industrial resources with such

"Atlanta Is Ours and Fairly Won" / 171

Vacated Rebel entrenchments overlooking one of the railroads leading from Atlanta.

Citizens of the city of Atlanta comply with Sherman's orders to evacuate the town.

Stone Mountain: The Confederate Mount Rushmore

Probably the most imposing and certainly the largest monument to the Confederacy is located 16 miles from Atlanta, Georgia. On Stone Mountain, the largest expanse of exposed granite on earth, is a three-acre carving of Southern icons Robert E. Lee, Thomas J. "Stonewall" Jackson and Jefferson Davis. While the idea for this great monument pre-dated the more famous work on Mount Rushmore, it was not actually completed until early in the 1970s. The troubled history of the carving on Stone Mountain was a long and drawn out affair of grand ambition, failed hopes and unshakable perseverance.

Stone Mountain itself is a 825 foot dome of igneous rock which was formed over 300 million years ago. It has remained an attraction since mankind first laid eyes on it. For the Indians who lived near the prominence, it was a mystical site. Spanish explorer Captain Juan Pardo was probably the first European to stumble on the mountain, back in the 16th century, while he was on a mission to build forts to protect Spanish Florida. Spying it from afar, he took its surface of feldspar, mica and quartz to be a mountain of rubies and diamonds. Pardo never got a chance to inspect Stone Mountain closely as attacks by Indians forced him to flee the area and he could not find speculators to finance a return trip once back in Florida. Later, long after the United States had come into existence, a enterprising fellow by the name of Aaron Cloud turned Stone Mountain into a tourist attraction, erecting a wooden tower on its summit and charging visitors $.50 for the view.

When the Georgia Railroad was built along its base, the mountain was effectively turned into a quarry. Stone Mountain did not figure prominently in the Civil War, but it did provide rock for the rebuilding of Atlanta after its destruction in the Atlanta campaign. Rock from Stone Mountain was also used to build municipal and commercial buildings throughout the United States and the world, including the U.S. Capitol Building, the Imperial Hotel in Tokyo, and the University of Havana. Pieces of Stone Mountain can also be found in such feats of engineering as the breakwaters for Charleston, South Carolina and New Orleans, Louisiana as well as the Panama Canal.

The idea for the construction of a Confederate monument at Stone Mountain was hatched in 1912 when Helen Pane, a member of the Atlanta chapter of the United Daughters of the Confederacy, conceived the idea of carving a bust of Robert E. Lee into the mountain as a memorial to the soldiers of the Confederacy. In 1915, Plane contacted noted sculptor Gutzon Borglum to execute the

Federal forces evacuating Atlanta to inaugurate the infamous March to the Sea.

project. When Borglum saw the mountain, his mind swam with grandiose ideas. He soon conceived a more ambitious plan which included a mounted Lee at the head of a massive legion of thousands of Southern soldiers. Taken by Borglum's plan, the United Daughters of the Confederacy formed a branch organization, known as the Stone Mountain Confederate Monumental Association, to manage the gargantuan project.

Borglum's connection with Stone Mountain was not to be a happy one. In 1916 the U.D.C. managed to win a deed for the northern face of the prominence from the mountain's owners, the Venable family. The proprietors of the mountain gave the organization 12 years to complete the memorial. World War I, financial problems and the immense practical difficulties which Borglum faced, delayed the inauguration of his project to be delayed until 1923. At last, Borglum commenced by using dynamite to blast away at the mountain side. On 19 January 1924, Borglum unveiled his first achievement to the public. Some 20,000 spectators, among them governors from several Southern states, came to see the completed carving of Lee's head. A celebration banquet was held on the granite shoulder of the carving. After this auspicious beginning, the relationship between Borglum and the U.D.C. began to sour and collapse. When, in 1925, the administrators attempted to make Borglum the scapegoat for continuing difficulties with the project, the sculptor grew incensed, destroyed his drawings and plans and escaped across the Georgia border, hotly pursued by a sheriff. Undaunted, Borglum went on to win fame for the construction of the National monument at Mount Rushmore.

The next sculptor to work on Stone Mountain was Augustus Lukeman. Lukeman abandoned Borglum's idea of a Confederate legion and decided to settle on figures of Lee, Jackson and Davis on horseback. In 1925, Borglum's work was blasted off the mountain and Lukeman started his attempt with workers using pneumatic drills. Three years later, the deadline for the project had passed with the work unfinished and the funds dried up. The Venable family reclaimed its property and the dream for a Confederate memorial at Stone Mountain faded for 36 years.

Fortunately, the hopes for Stone Mountain did not disappear completely. In 1958, the mountain and the surrounding area was purchased by the state of Georgia. The concept of the Confederate Memorial was resurrected through the Stone Mountain Memorial Association, and the Stone Mountain Memorial Advisory Committee created by the Georgia General Assembly. In 1963, the committee selected Walter K. Hancock to complete Lukeman's work, which was little more than an outline when the project was dropped in 1928. From 1964 to 1972, Hancock and his crew worked with thermo-jet torches to carve the figures out of the rock. In 1970, Vice President Spiro T. Agnew presided over a commemoration ceremony for the work, and two years later the project was finally completed.

The Stone Mountain memorial is a wonder in itself. Larger than a football field, 90 feet tall and 190 feet wide, it is the largest piece of bas-relief art in the world.

174 / THE ATLANTA CAMPAIGN

a singleness of purpose that the Confederacy would be severely crippled. By November, Sherman's planned march was ready to be put into effect. Sherman fired what was left of Atlanta and moved off for Savannah and the sea.

As Sherman and his army headed for the Georgia coast, one significant failure of his campaign was plain for all to see. One of his major objectives had been to destroy the Army of Tennessee and, although he dealt it numerous defeats, the force still existed to take to the field and fight once again. As long as the Army of Tennessee was still active, the war would continue, many more men would die in battle, and civilians would continue to suffer the depredations of invading armies.

However, in all other respects, the campaign was undeniably successful. Sherman had accomplished his other objective, to seriously damage the resources of the Confederate war machine; Atlanta's factories, railroads and storehouses were of no further use to the Confederacy, and soon all of Georgia and most of the Carolinas would be knocked out of the fight. Sherman's campaigns, though they showed little in the way of tactical prowess, demonstrated the general's remarkable strategic sense. During his tenure in command, the general had become dedicated to destroying the Confederate capacity to sustain its armies in the field and exhausting the will of a nation to fight. The grim Federal warrior approached these tasks with almost maniacal devotion which has seldom been seen since in the annals of American warfare.

The wake of Sherman's army during the march to the sea: stragglers and enslaved persons.

Bibliography

*U*nfortunately, there are few adequate discussions of the Atlanta campaign available to readers at the present time. An older work, *Atlanta* (New York: 1882) by Jacob D. Cox, is the standard piece though its language and presentation are dated and somewhat difficult to understand. A more modern and readable account is *War So Terrible* (New York: 1987) by James Lee McDonough and James Pickett Jones which served as a helpful source for this book. However, by far the best accounts of the Atlanta campaign to date are not to be found in a book, but in the *Blue & Gray* magazine series on the subject. The articles found in the three-issue series, by some of the leading historians on the battles fought place for Atlanta, and are well-written and very informative. They are listed in the bibliography below. The best compilation of primary source material is *The Atlanta Papers* (Dayton, Ohio: 1980) edited by Sydney C. Kerksis. All these works and those listed below were instrumental in the preparation of this volume.

Black, Samuel. *A Soldier's Recollections of the Civil War.* (Minco, Oklahoma: 1911-1912.)

Brown, Edmund R. *The 27th Indiana Volunteer Infantry in the War of the Rebellion.*

Brown, Joseph M. *The Mountain Campaigns in Georgia* (Buffalo, New York: 1890.)

Chipman, N. P. *The Tragedy of Andersonville.* (Sacramento, California: 1911.)

Connelly, Thomas L. *Autumn of Glory: The Army of the Tennessee.* (Baton Rouge: 1971)

Conyngham, David P. *Sherman's March Through the South.* (New York: 1865.)

Buel, Clarence C. and Robert U. Johnson eds. *Battles and Leaders of the Civil War.* (New York: 1888.)

Davis, Stephen. "Atlanta Campaign: Hood Fights Desperately. The Battles of Atlanta. Actions From July 10 to September 2, 1864." *Blue & Gray.* (August, 1989.)

Davis, Stephen. "Pat Cleburne's Emancipation Proposal." *Blue & Gray.* (April 1989.)

Dictionary of Literary Biography. (Detroit, Michigan: 1981.)

Drake, George. *The Mail Goes Through.* (San Angelo, Texas: 1964.)

Faust, Patricia L., ed. *Historical Times Illustrated Encyclopedia of the Civil War.* (New York: 1986.)

Futch, Ovid L. *History of Andersonville Prison.* Gainesville, Florida: 1968.)

Hagerman, Edward. *The American Civil War and the Origins of Modern Warfare.* (Bloomington, Illinois: 1988.)

Hanson, Elizabeth I. *Margaret Mitchell* (Boston.)

Hattaway, Herman and Archer Jones. *How the North Won.* (Urbana, Illinois: 1983.)

Head, Thomas A. *Campaigns and Battles of the Sixteenth Regiment Tennessee Volunteers.* (Nashville.)

Heseltine, William B. *Civil War Prisons.* (New York: 1964.)

Hinkley, Julian W. *A Narrative of Service with the Third Wisconsin Infantry.* (1912)

Hoehling, A. A. *Last Train from Atlanta.* (New York: 1956)

Hood, John B. *Advance and Retreat.* (Bloomington, 1952)

Horn, Stanley F. *The Army of Tennessee.* (Norman, Oklahoma: 1952)

Jackson, Oscar L. *The Colonel's Diary.* (Sharon, Pa: 1922)

Jameson, Matthew H. *Recollections of Pioneer and Army Life.* (Kansas City: 1911.)

Johnson, Andrew J. *The Civil War Diary of Andrew Jackson Johnson.*

Johnston, Joseph E. *Narrative of Military Operations.* (Bloomington, Indiana: 1952)

Kelly, Dennis. "Atlanta Campaign: Mountains to Pass, A River to Cross. The Battle of Kennesaw Mountain, and Related Actions from June 10 to July 9, 1864." *Blue & Gray.* (June 1989.)

Kurtz, Wilbur G. *The Atlanta Cyclorama.* (Atlanta: 1953)

Lewis, Whitsel. *A Union Soldier's Diary.* (St. Louis, 1964.)

McMurry, Richard M. "Atlanta Campaign: Rocky Face Ridge to the Dallas Line, the Battles of May 1864." *Blue & Gray.* (April 1989.)

McMurry, Richard M. *John Bell Hood and the War for Southern Independence.* (Louisville: 1982.)

McPherson, James M. *Battle Cry of Freedom.* (New York: 1988.)

Miles, Jim. *Fields of Glory.* (Nashville: 1989.)

Nash, Jay Robert and Stanley Ralph Ross. *The Motion Picture Guide.* (Chicago: 1986)

Nofi, Albert A. *Civil War Treasury.* (New York: 1990.)

Paver, John M. *What I Saw from 1861-1864.*

Ridley, Bromfield L. *Battles and Sketches of the Army of Tennessee.* (Mexico, Missouri: 1906.)

Sears, Stephen. *George B. McClellan: The Young Napoleon.* (New York: 1988.)

Shelton, Morris. *Georgia's Piece of the Rock.* (Atlanta.)

Smith, Benjamin T. *Private Smith's Journal.* (Chicago: 1963.)

Smith, W. B. *On Wheels and How I Came There.* (New York: 1893.)

Thosburn, Thomas C. *My Experiences During the Civil War.* (Cleveland, Ohio: 1963)

Tourgee, Albon W. *The Story of a Thousand.* (Buffalo, New York: 1896.)

Turner, George E. *Victory Rode the Rails.* Westport, Connecticutt: 1972.)

United States Congress. Report No. 65. (Washington, D.C., 1864.)

Young, Lot D. *Reminiscences of a Soldier of the Orphan Brigade.* (Paris, Kentucky.)

War of the Rebellion Official Records. Series 1, Vol. 38. (Washington, D.C.: 1891)

Watkins, Sam R. *Co. Aytch, Maury Grays, 1st Tennessee Regiment or A Sideshow for a Bigshow.* (Nashville: 1882.)

Woodworth, Steven E. *Jefferson Davis and His Generals.* (Lawrence, Kansas: 1990.)

W
22.45

PETTIGREW REGIONAL LIBRARY